The Creative Hooker

Jessie A. Turbayne

Schiffer Publishing Ltd

4880 Lower Valley Road, Atglen, Pennsylvania 19310

Dedication

With love to: Rob and Molly

Title page photo, center:
"English Garden." W. Cushing and Company pattern. Hooked by Patricia J. Chambers. 2003. 38.5" x 46". *Courtesy of Patricia J. Chambers.*

Title page photo, bottom:
"Bacon and Eggs." Pris Buttler Rug Designs pattern. Hooked by Jacque Smith. Missouri. 2004. 30" x 36". *Courtesy of Jacque Smith.*

"Tea and Oranges." Designed and hooked by Trish Johnson. Ontario, Canada. 2004. 18.5" x 19.5". *Courtesy of Trish Johnson.*

Other Schiffer Books by Jessie A. Turbayne
Hooked on Rugs: Outstanding Contemporary Designs
The Big Book of Hooked Rugs: 1950-1980s
The Complete Guide to Collecting Hooked Rugs: Unrolling the Secrets
The Hooker's Art: Evolving Designs in Hooked Rugs
Hooked Rug Treasury

Other Schiffer Books on Related Subjects
Hooked Rugs Today: Strong Women, Flowers, Animals, Children, Christmas, Miniatures, and More - 2006, by Amy Oxford
Punch Needle Rug Hooking: Techniques and Designs, by Amy Oxford
Contemporary Hooked Rugs: Themes and Memories, by Linda Rae Coughlin

Library of Congress Cataloging-in-Publication Data

Turbayne, Jessie A.
   The creative hooker / Jessie Turbayne.
      p. cm.
   ISBN 978-0-7643-2645-5 (hardcover)
   1. Rugs, Hooked--United States--Catalogs. 2. Rugs, Hooked--Canada--Catalogs. I. Title.

NK2812.T8698 2007
746.7'40433--dc22

                    2007007622

Designed by "Sue"
Type set in Zapf Humanist Demi BT/Novarese Bk BT

ISBN: 978-0-7643-2645-5
Printed in China

Published by Schiffer Publishing Ltd.
4880 Lower Valley Road
Atglen, PA 19310
Phone: (610) 593-1777; Fax: (610) 593-2002
E-mail: Info@schifferbooks.com

For the largest selection of fine reference books on this and related subjects, please visit our web site at
www.schifferbooks.com
We are always looking for people to write books on new and related subjects. If you have an idea for a book please contact us at the above address.

This book may be purchased from the publisher.
Include $3.95 for shipping.
Please try your bookstore first.
You may write for a free catalog.

In Europe, Schiffer books are distributed by
Bushwood Books
6 Marksbury Ave.
Kew Gardens
Surrey TW9 4JF England
Phone: 44 (0) 20 8392-8585; Fax: 44 (0) 20 8392-9876
E-mail: info@bushwoodbooks.co.uk
Website: www.bushwoodbooks.co.uk
Free postage in the U.K., Europe; air mail at cost.

Contents

Above:
"Visiting Kitten." Designed by Victoria Hart Ingalls. Victoria Hart Ingalls pattern. Hooked by Dorothy Rezac. Kansas.1996. 8.5" x 11". *Courtesy of Dorothy Rezac.*

Acknowledgments

I wish to extend my sincere gratitude to those who contributed to the making of this book:

A very special word of thanks to my editor, Donna Baker, and Schiffer Publishing Ltd.

Heartfelt appreciation to:

All the rug hooking artists, north and south of the border, who so kindly shared their work and enthusiasm.

Michael, after all these years…you're still the one.

Jamie, who started all of this over three decades ago when you handed me an old holey rug and suggested I fix it. Thank you for teaching me so much.

Judy Yasi, for your friendship, keen mind, professional insight, and for continuing the daunting job of trying to bring me into the world of technology and doing so with patience and humor.

To Francesca Rossi Lehman, thank you for your love, friendship, and introducing me to Federal Hill and espresso.

Kind acknowledgements: Susan Andreson; Jeanne Benjamin; The Carnegie Center for Art and History, New Albany, Indiana; Terry Dorr; The Dorr Mill Store, Guild, New Hampshire; John and Nancy Ewbank; Jeanne Field; Chris Gooding, Tom and Victoria Ingalls; Trish Johnson; Carolyn Kilner; Roslyn Logsdon; Shirley Lyons and the Georgetown Rug Hooking Guild; Margaret Arraj MacDonald; Marge Mello; Sherry Paisley; The Potted Pear, West Chester, Ohio; Suzi Prather; Rittermere-Hurst-Field, Aurora, Ontario, Canada; Jenny Rupp; Eric Sandberg; Gene Shepherd; Annie A. Spring; Tricia Travis; Cindy Trick; C. Allan Turbayne; Justina Rae Two Eagle; Patricia Yearout Wharton and Lisa Yeago.

"Thistle." Designed and hooked by Kim Nixon. Tennessee. 2001. 24.5" x 36". *Courtesy of Kim Nixon.*

Introduction

When word got out that I was thinking of doing a book focusing only on recently made hooked rugs (those created in the past ten years), the response from rug hookers across the United States, Canada, and beyond was overwhelming. Hundreds of spirited rug hookers showed up at photo shoots, arms laden with samples of their work. Thousands of photos, negatives, slides, and digital images were sent to my Westwood, Massachusetts studio. What originally was intended to be one book has become two. *Hooked on Rugs: Outstanding Contemporary Designs*, released in the summer of 2006, was received by an enthusiastic audience. Here, complete with 500 plus images, is the second half of the series, *The Creative Hooker*. Sit down, relax, and enjoy the best that today's rug hookers have to offer.

Note: Hooked rug measurements have been rounded to the nearest half inch. All rugs are hooked on burlap, rug hooking linen, monk's cloth, cotton warp, or other foundations using cut strips of woolen fabric unless noted. In some cases of special interest, the hooking materials have been listed. Using information supplied by rug owners as well as my own research, all efforts have been made to properly identify rug hookers, titles of their work, dates of completion, dimensions, and names of patterns and pattern makers. The author claims no responsibility for any misidentification. All hooked pieces adapted from the work of other artists were done so with permission. Permission was obtained by the hooking artist and not the author. The author claims no responsibility for any copyright infringements.

"Phoenix of Peace." Designed by Pearl McGown. W. Cushing and Company pattern. Hooked by Roland C. Nunn. California. 2004. 28" x 22". *Courtesy of Roland C. Nunn.*

"Drag-On-Fly." Designed and hooked by Sharon Saknit. California. 2003. 13" x 13". *Courtesy of Sharon Saknit.*

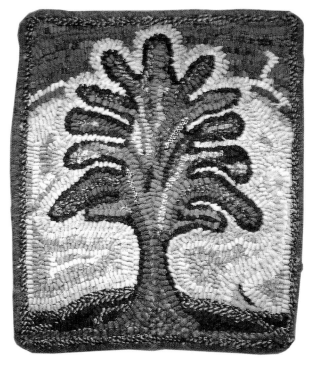

"Campfire." Designed and hooked by Kathy T. Stephens. Montana. 2003. 11" x 9". *Courtesy of Kathy T. Stephens.*

"Portrait Lady." Designed by Victoria Hart Ingalls. Victoria Hart Ingalls pattern. Hooked by Lorraine Beaver. Missouri. 1996. 16" x 20". *Courtesy of Lorraine Beaver.*

Wonder Woman…Deanie Pass

"Hmm…I Wonder." Part of a series of rugs in which sculptress turned rug hooker, Deanie Pass, imagines herself in another role. In this case she is transformed into cartoon and television character "Wonder Woman." Designed and hooked by Deanie Pass. Minnesota. 2005. 18" x 26". *Courtesy of Deanie Pass.*

A Tribute to Emily Carr

On Inspiration…What do I want to express? The subject means little. The arrangement, the design, colour, shape, depth, light, space, mood, movement, balance, not one of all these fills the bill. There is something additional, a breath that draws your breath into breathing, a heartbeat that pounds on yours, a recognition of the oneness of all things.

—Emily Carr

Emily Carr (1871-1945) was a well-known Canadian artist who also hooked rugs. Born in gold-rush frontier Victoria the year British Columbia became a province, Emily studied art in the United States, England, and France. With palette and brush in hand, she returned to, and spent much of her life in her Vancouver Island homeland surrounded by the lush environment and Native people that inspired many of Carr's most beloved paintings—paintings that would help define Canadian art.

During the lean years of World War I, in addition to selling paintings and being a landlord, the multi-talented and resourceful Carr sold sheep dogs, her own Native inspired pottery, and rugs that she designed and hooked.

With today's increasing international interest in Canadian art, Ontario's Rittermere-Hurst-Field, purveyors of rug hooking supplies, has obtained permission from the British Columbia Archives to reproduce several of Carr's paintings and designs in the form of pre-printed rug hooking patterns. Met with great enthusiasm by rug hookers and hooked rug admirers, Emily Carr's work lives on.

What follows is a sampling of several hooked likenesses of Carr's paintings and surviving hooked rugs. In most instances, the colors used by the hooking artists replicate those used by Carr.

"Street Scene, Alert Bay" depicts Vancouver Island Natives gathered around a magnificently carved totem pole. Choosing a palette similar to Emily Carr's, Marnie Cormack uses her hook and strips of woolen fabric to recreate the artist's brush strokes. Adapted from a painting by Canadian artist Emily Carr. Rittermere-Hurst-Field pattern with permission of British Columbia Archives Call No. PDP00559. Hooked by Marnie Cormack. Ontario, Canada. 2004. 20" x 16". *Courtesy of Marnie Cormack.*

Carved from tree trunks and erected near Native Northwestern tribal houses, totem poles served as emblems of family or clan and often represented mythical historical incidents. This hooked "Kitwanger Pole" replicates Carr's lively color scheme. Adapted from a painting by Canadian artist Emily Carr. Rittermere-Hurst-Field pattern with permission of British Columbia Archives Call No. PDP00585. Hooked by Marnie Cormack. Ontario, Canada. 2004. 20" x 13". *Courtesy of Marnie Cormack.*

The deceased look down upon the living. "Sechelt Strait of Georgia." Adapted from a painting by Canadian artist Emily Carr. Rittermere-Hurst-Field pattern with permission of British Columbia Archives Call No. PDP00827. Hooked by Marnie Cormack. Ontario, Canada. 2005. 12" x 20". *Courtesy of Marnie Cormack.*

A village scene of "Sitka at the Bakery and Shops of the Russians." Adapted from a painting by Canadian artist Emily Carr. Rittermere-Hurst-Field pattern with permission of the British Archives Call No PDP00660. Hooked by Marnie Cormack. Ontario, Canada. 2005. 17" x 24". *Courtesy of Marnie Cormack.*

"Sombreness Sunlit." The juxtaposition of light and dark values enhances the feeling of leaving a wooded area and entering a sun drenched clearing. Adapted from a painting by Canadian artist Emily Carr. Rittermere-Hurst-Field pattern with permission of British Archives Call No. PDP00633. Hooked by Marnie Cormack. Ontario, Canada. 2005. 20" x 12". *Courtesy of Marnie Cormack.*

Inspired by one of Carr's hooked rugs, Marnie Cormack crafted her "Eagle Rug" with traditional "Haida (Northwestern Native tribe) colours and added motifs." Adapted from a hooked rug by Canadian artist Emily Carr. Rittermere-Hurst-Field pattern with permission of British Archives Call No. PDP01540. Hooked by Marnie Cormack. Ontario, Canada. 2004. 34" x 43". *Courtesy of Marnie Cormack.*

Emerging from the earth in the lush Garden of Eden, "Adam and Eve" reach out to one another. Adapted from a hooked rug by Canadian artist Emily Carr. Rittermere-Hurst-Field pattern with permission of British Archives Call No. PDP03665. Hooked by Georgia Hall. Ontario, Canada. 2005. 15" x 50". *Courtesy of Georgia Hall.*

Hooked planes of color created an impressionistic forest. "Painters and Painting." Adapted from a painting by Canadian artist Emily Carr. Rittermere-Hurst-Field pattern with permission of British Columbia Archives Call No. PDP00931. Hooked by Georgia Hall. Ontario, Canada. 2005. 16" x 17". *Courtesy of Georgia Hall.*

"Woo," a portrait of Emily Carr's pet monkey. Adapted from a painting by Canadian artist Emily Carr. Rittermere-Hurst-Field pattern with permission of British Columbia Archives Call No. PDP00603. Hooked by Georgia Hall. Ontario, Canada. 2004. 20" x 12". *Courtesy of Georgia Hall.*

"Skagway From End of the Wharf." Calm waters, hooked with subtly changing shades, reflect the colors of the sky and nearby landscape. Adapted from a painting by Canadian artist Emily Carr. Rittermere-Hurst-Field pattern with permission of British Archives Call No. PDP00562. Hooked by Georgia Hall. Ontario, Canada. 2005. 13" x 17". *Courtesy of Georgia Hall.*

Rittermere-Hurst-Field – Aurora, Ontario, Canada

With family traditions rich in rug hooking, Rittermere-Hurst-Field is the company many Canadians and Americans turn to when they need supplies. Founded in the 1960s by Margaret and Ted Rowan, the popular company was purchased by Jeanne Hurst Field in 1984 and continues to operate under her astute guidance and that of her friendly and capable staff. Their catalogue, *The RHF Book of Designs*, offers a wide variety of pre-printed patterns, including the designs of several Canadian artists such as David Rankine, George Culley, Shelley Atkinson, and Emily Carr.

Right and far right, top: A visit to Rittermere-Hurst-Field, "Canada's Centre for rug hooking designs and supplies." *Photos courtesy of Michelle Dunn and Rittermere-Hurst-Field.*

A color plan, woolen fabrics, and hooked work in progress. *Photos courtesy of Michelle Dunn and Rittermere-Hurst-Field.*

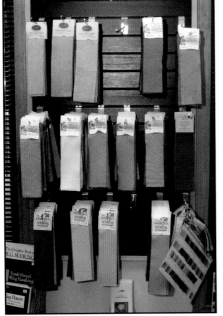

Not only does Rittermere-Hurst-Field offer rug hooking patterns for sale, they can show you the finished product. *Photo courtesy of Michelle Dunn and Rittermere-Hurst-Field.*

Rug hookers like to use a wide variety of swatches and hand-dyed woolen fabrics. *Photos courtesy of Michelle Dunn and Rittermere-Hurst-Field.*

The Georgetown Rug Hooking Guild – Ontario, Canada

Founded in 1968, the Georgetown branch of the Ontario Hooking Craft Guild has an active and growing membership. The group meets monthly for workshops and to hear invited speakers. Yearly, the one hundred or so members work on a group project, sponsor a display of their work, and share their love of rug hooking with each other and anyone interested in learning the craft.

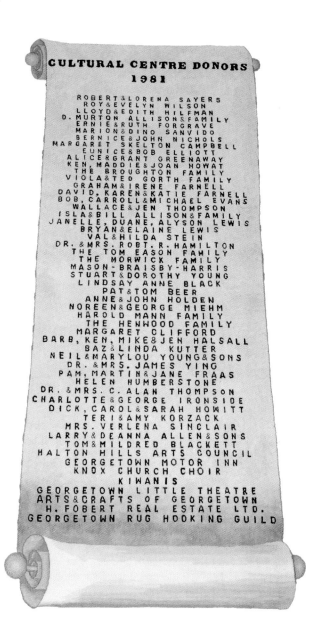

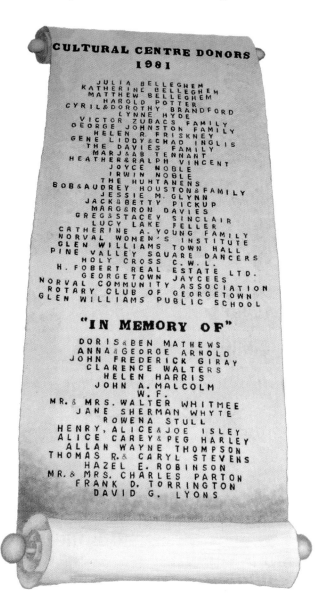

Every two years, the Georgetown Rug Hooking Guild displays over one hundred hooked works of art in the gallery of the local Cultural Centre. In 1981, the guild was asked to help raise funds for the Centre's theatre. Members hooked two banners, each nine feet by five feet, containing the names of those who purchased space on the hangings. Known as the "Monsters," the hefty projects were passed among the talented rug makers until the job was completed, then hung in the Cultural Centre for all to see. *Courtesy of the Georgetown Rug Hooking Guild.*

Hooked by members of the Georgetown Guild, "Zereh" was used as a lucky draw fund raising first prize. "To our shock, the winner didn't have any shades of blue in her home and sold the rug to a member of our guild." Designed by Jane McGown Flynn. House of Price / Charco pattern. Hooked by members of the Georgetown Rug Hooking Guild. Ontario, Canada. 1996. 36" x 56". *Courtesy of Gwen Brierley and the Georgetown Rug Hooking Guild.*

Upon presentation of this special rug, these words of gratitude were given: "Grateful members of the Georgetown branch of the Ontario Hooking Craft Guild hooked this rug for Shirley Lyons in acknowledgment of her tireless and generous contributions to the world of rug hooking for over thirty-five years. It is a small tribute to someone who has given so much to promote our craft, but it was hooked with great affection. It is truly a story rug, with motifs depicting some of the most important interests of Shirley's busy life. There are rug patterns, wool, and dye pots to acknowledge her innovative techniques, and a hook and shaded rose representing the legions of beginners that have learned to hook in her classes. Note the PFAFF machine logo that gives a nod to her sewing and quilting classes, and a teddy, because her bear classes have produced heirloom quality teddies and the unique beaded purse pendants she creates in her 'spare time.' Finally, the heraldic lion (rampant) seen at the bottom of the rug, depicts not only her amazingly strong personality and outlook on life, but her own personal 'Lyons' logo." "Hookers' Folk Life Oriental." Designed by Ingrid Hieronimus and added to by the Georgetown Rug Hooking Guild. Hooked by members of the Georgetown Rug Hooking Guild. Ontario, Canada. 2002. 44" x 28". Courtesy of the Georgetown Rug Hooking Guild and Shirley Lyons.

Shirley Lyons and the Georgetown Rug Hooking Guild are synonymous. Thanks to her tireless efforts and enthusiasm, dedication, and unquestionable skill, many have come to know the joys of rug hooking.

A masterfully hooked ribbon twists around a linear border framing "Regal Rose." Blossoms and buds, hooked with gradation swatches, each with ten values, are complemented by thirty-six leaves. Designed by Jane McGown Flynn. House of Price / Charco pattern. Hooked by Shirley Lyons. Ontario, Canada. 2003. 44" x 30". *Courtesy of Shirley Lyons.*

A portion of the aforementioned "Regal Rose" was utilized as a monochromatic study. Using woolen fabric, Shirley Lyons hand-dyed ten value swatches with shades ranging from dark gray to white. Black beads embellish the wall hanging's dyed woolen fabric frame. Designed by Jane McGown Flynn. House of Price / Charco pattern. Hooked by Shirley Lyons. Ontario, Canada. 2004. 26" x 20". *Courtesy of Shirley Lyons.*

The same portion of the "Regal Rose" pattern sports a different look. Designed by Jane McGown Flynn. House of Price/ Charco pattern. Hooked by Shirley Lyons. Ontario, Canada. 2003. 26" x 20". *Courtesy of Shirley Lyons.*

Why not carry hooked art? Artist and teacher Shirley Lyons took the challenge and not only dyed the woolen fabric used to hook "Qashqai Kilim Tote Bag" (shown front and back), she also dyed the suede trim and handles. Designed by Jane McGown. House of Price / Charco pattern. Hooked by Shirley Lyons. Ontario, Canada. 1999. 20" x 22". *Courtesy of Shirley Lyons.*

"A lion hooked for my Lyons' Den Hooking Studio," complete with a decorative edge braided with the fabric used to hook the outer background. "Lion Primitive." W. Cushing and Company pattern. Hooked by Shirley Lyons. Ontario, Canada. 1997. 31" x 56". *Courtesy of Shirley Lyons.*

"Who says we can only hook rugs? This hanging was hooked to frame photos of my grandchildren. Now another boy has been added, so I must do another frame for him." Designed by Helen Barrett. Hooked by Shirley Lyons. Ontario, Canada. 2002. 8" x 8". *Courtesy of Shirley Lyons.*

Members' Gallery

Using her hook and strips of woolen fabric, tribute is paid to English poet, artist, and socialist William Morris (1834-1896) in this reverse image of "Rabbits and Tulips." Rittermere-Hurst-Field pattern. Hooked by Jennifer Arruda. Ontario, Canada. 2005. 26.5" x 38.5". *Courtesy of Jennifer Arruda.*

"This is the first rug I designed myself. 'Madigan' is a soft-coated wheaten terrier. The shamrocks in the corners of the rug are a tribute to the Irish heritage of the breed and the maple leaves reflect the fact that we live in Canada." Designed and hooked by Jennifer Arruda. Ontario, Canada. 2000. 35.5" x 42". *Courtesy of Jennifer Arruda.*

The subtle background of "Queen's Circle" was achieved by spot-dyeing woolen fabric with a "wash" of the colors used to hook the flowers. Rittermere-Hurst-Field pattern. Hooked by Jennifer Arruda. Ontario, Canada. 2005. Diameter 38.5". *Courtesy of Jennifer Arruda.*

"I designed this rug for what was supposed to be a 'proddy rug' workshop but I found that I preferred hooking the loops up high and clipping them later to give my dog and the grass a shaggy look. I call this rug 'Waiting for Joe' because the only time Madigan would lie still long enough for me to take a picture, let alone design a rug of her, was when she'd lie in the shade under the red maple tree on the front lawn and wait for my husband to return home from work." Designed and hooked by Jennifer Arruda. Ontario, Canada. 2002. 21" x 29". *Courtesy of Jennifer Arruda.*

"When it came to hooking the sky on this antique pattern, I was stumped. My teacher, Shirley Lyons, came to the rescue and painted dye onto wool to produce the perfect colors for hooking a brilliant sunset. I modified the pattern slightly. When I had just a small area remaining in the left hand corner of the rug, I laid it on the floor to have a better look at it. My wheaten terrier came galloping in from the outside covered in balls of snow and flopped down on my rug to thaw out. I couldn't resist hooking Madigan with snowballs intact, into that little remaining space on the rug." Eaton's rug pattern. Hooked by Jennifer Arruda. Ontario, Canada. 2002. 26" x 48". *Courtesy of Jennifer Arruda.*

"A Woodsy Greeting" was adapted from an antique Christmas card. Hooked by Jennifer Arruda. Ontario, Canada. 2004. 26" x 39". *Courtesy of Jennifer Arruda.*

"I have a great interest in lettering, so I chose this style for the word "Welcome" because the hanging was to be displayed in a large, old, formal Victorian house. It looks very much at home in the entrance hallway." Designed and hooked by Helen Barrett. Ontario, Canada. 2001. 20" x 28.5". *Courtesy of Helen Barrett.*

Oval wreaths of simple posies surround a trio of roses. "The old pattern had an attached label bearing the name 'Peony.' Try as I might, I cannot identify a peony—they look like roses to me!" Dritz pattern. Hooked by Helen Barrett. Ontario, Canada. 2001. 34.5" x 50". *Courtesy of Helen Barrett.*

To achieve the effects of light coming through a stained glass window, Anne Boissinot hooked "Lilies of the Pond" with 6/32" and 8/32" wide strips of hand-dyed woolen fabric, including specially dyed "copper foil." The "foil" surrounds each design element and forms the rug's outer edge. Designed by Sharon Britt. House of Price / Charco pattern. Hooked by Anne Boissinot. Ontario, Canada. 2003. 29" x 44". *Courtesy of Anne Boissinot.*

A visit to Turkey's "Anatolian Borders." Hand-dyed woolen fabrics were used to create the soft pastel images, background field, and borders. Designed by Jane McGown Flynn. House of Price / Charco pattern. Hooked by Anne Boissinot. Ontario, Canada. 2003. 24" x 36". *Courtesy of Anne Boissinot.*

ATHA, the Association of Traditional Hooking Artists, held their 2005 biennial in scenic Nova Scotia. When asked to hook an historical building in Halifax, rug hooking artist and teacher Anne Boissinot chose "the Old Town Clock," which sits high on Citadel Hill overlooking the port city. Fourteen values of white were used to hook the octagonal structure, and a functioning clock movement was added. Nova Scotia's tartan frames the postcard image. Designed and hooked by Anne Boissinot. Ontario, Canada. 2005. 22" x 16". *Courtesy of Anne Boissinot.*

Simplistic "Tulips," formed from solid planes of color, offer an uplifting note of cheer. Rittermere-Hurst-Field pattern. Hooked by Gwen Brierley. Ontario, Canada. 1996. 36" x 19". *Courtesy of Gwen Brierley.*

A decorative William Morris motif inspired "Leaves and Flowers." Designed by Doris Norman. Hooked by Gail Bukata. Ontario, Canada. 2004. 37" x 36". *Courtesy 0f Gail Bukata.*

Framed by an Azeri-style border, "Gabbeh," honors woven story telling tribal carpets. Designed by Jane McGown Flynn. House of Price / Charco pattern. Hooked by Gwen Brierley. Ontario, Canada. 1998. 24" x 35". *Courtesy of Gwen Brierley.*

This wall hanging depicting "Celtic Lions" was hooked for a son-in-law of similar heritage. Adapted from an image found in a needlework book. Hooked by Gail Bukata. Ontario, Canada. 2005. 16" x 24". *Courtesy of Gail Bukata.*

"Maple Leaves - Blue Nose # 2072." Based in Nova Scotia, Garrett's Blue Nose, with British, American, as well as Canadian distributors, designed, printed, and sold rug hooking patterns from 1892 until 1974. Copyrights were recently purchased and the popular designs are once again available to hooking enthusiasts. Garrett's Blue Nose rug pattern. Hooked by Gail Bukata. Ontario, Canada. 2004. 17" x 28". *Courtesy of Gail Bukata.*

"Antoinette" brings together fanciful flowers, foliage, and fine-feathered fowl. Rittermere-Hurst-Field pattern. Hooked by Gwen Brierley. Ontario, Canada. 1995. 38" x 17". *Courtesy of Gwen Brierley.*

A favorite traditional pattern from days gone by. Even distribution of colors makes for a visually pleasing rug. Name of pattern and pattern maker unknown. Hooked by Gail Bukata. Ontario, Canada. 2003. 21.5" x 37.5". *Courtesy of Gail Bukata.*

Entered into *Monochromatic*, a juried fiber exhibit, "X's and O's" was fashioned after images of crosses in a church's stained glass window. Designed and hooked by Gail Bukata. Ontario, Canada. 2004. 21.5" x 34". *Courtesy of Gail Bukata.*

"Thanksgiving in Palgrave" replicates the "fall colours of my childhood hometown." Designed and hooked by Bonnie Charter. Ontario, Canada. 2004. 30" x 56". *Courtesy of Bonnie Charter.*

"Rapture," a glorious gathering of blossoms large and small. "This rug allowed me to learn many new ways to dye wool." Designed by Jane McGown Flynn. House of Price / Charco pattern. Hooked by Bonnie Charter. Ontario, Canada. 2001. 43" x 80". *Courtesy of Bonnie Charter.*

"Kilim Trent," named for the Trent Rug Hooking School, combines figural and geometric elements. The background of this Oriental-style rug was horizontally hooked to mimic its woven counterpart. Designed and hooked by Ruby Clarke. Ontario, Canada. 2004. 30" x 52". *Courtesy of Ruby Clarke.*

This "Tree of Life Crewel" employs creative hooking stitches of reverse background, turkey work, chain, and seed stitch. Karlkraft pattern. Hooked by Carolyn Clemens. Ontario, Canada. 2002. 28" x 16". *Courtesy of Carolyn Clemens.*

"Duchess Crewel" was fashioned using creative hooking stitches including reverse background, sculpturing, chain, and seed stitch. Designed by Jane McGown Flynn. House of Price / Charco pattern. Hooked by Carolyn Clemens. Ontario, Canada. 2005. 22" x 36". *Courtesy of Carolyn Clemens.*

"Peking" reminds us of lush silk fabrics from exotic lands. Heirloom Rugs pattern. Hooked by Carolyn Clemens. Ontario, Canada. 2002. 44" x 72". *Courtesy of Carolyn Clemens.*

"Rapture Plus Four." A banner of beautiful blossoms recalls summer days. Note the fine shading throughout. Designed by Jane McGown Flynn. House of Price / Charco pattern. Hooked by Carolyn Clemens. Ontario, Canada. 2005. 14" x 60". *Courtesy of Carolyn Clemens.*

"Anatolian Runner" melds architectural and decorative motifs. Hooking in a horizontal manner using "abrashed" or mottled hand-dyed woolen fabrics mimics tonal color changes often found in the background field of woven carpets. Designed by Jane McGown Flynn. House of Price / Charco pattern. Hooked by Nancy Cook. Ontario, Canada. 2005. 30" x 72". *Courtesy of Nancy Cook.*

A flower lined path leads to an imaginary "Culley's Cottage." During the mid 1930s, artist George Culley designed and sold hooked rug patterns to Canada's popular Eaton's department store. George Culley Collection. Rittermere-Hurst-Field pattern. Hooked by Carolyn Clemens. Ontario, Canada. 2004. 24" x 27". *Courtesy of Carolyn Clemens.*

"Juliet's Crewel" features fanciful flowers and foliage hooked in authentic crewel embroidery colors. Designed by Jane McGown Flynn. House of Price / Charco pattern. Hooked by Jean Crocker. Ontario, Canada. 2004. 44" x 24". *Courtesy of Jean Crocker.*

A stylized "Tree of Life," is complemented by a stylized floral and diamond jewel-like border. Rittermere-Hurst-Field pattern. Hooked by Nancy Cook. Ontario, Canada. 2003. 37" x 31". *Courtesy of Nancy Cook*

"Kilim," hooked with woolen fabric hand-dyed by the artist, pays tribute to woven story-telling carpets. It was crafted with strips cut 4/32" wide, with the exception of the "flecks of colour" that were 2/32" wide. For authenticity, a braided fringe was added. Designed and hooked by Barbara J. D'Arcy. Ontario, Canada. 1997. 18" x 55". *Courtesy of Barbara J. D'Arcy.*

Blending an old design with modern colors, "Priscilla" boasts an array of folk art flowers hooked from woolen fabric hand-dyed by the rug maker. Designed by Joan Moshimer. W. Cushing and Company pattern. Hooked by Barbara J. D'Arcy. Ontario, Canada. 2000. 32" x 58". *Courtesy of Barbara J. D'Arcy.*

Colorful "Chinese Butterflies," of all sizes, flutter about a neutral horizontally hooked background. A traditional Oriental cloud design forms the decorative border. Designed by Jane McGown Flynn. House of Price / Charco pattern. Hooked by Margaret Ewing. Ontario, Canada. 2005. 24" x 48". *Courtesy of Margaret Ewing.*

"Persian Gardens" was adapted from a sixteenth century Levantine design. Ancient Arabic-like characters, of an imagined origin, complement this hooked prayer rug. Rittermere-Hurst-Field pattern. Hooked by Margaret Ewing. Ontario, Canada. 2001. 90" x 48". *Courtesy of Margaret Ewing.*

A hooked collage of leisure activities is found in "Cottage Country." Rittermere-Hurst-Field pattern. Hooked by Gail Finlayson. Ontario, Canada. 2001. 51" x 33". *Courtesy of Gail Finlayson.*

Knotted or hooked? Rug hookers are a clever and ingenious lot and often hook rugs that imitate woven and knotted Oriental carpets. Named for a region in Western Turkey, "Anatolia" offers authentic coloration, pleasing geometric design, and added fringe. Rittermere-Hurst-Field pattern. Hooked by Gail Finlayson. Ontario, Canada. 2002. 26" x 49". *Courtesy of Gail Finlayson.*

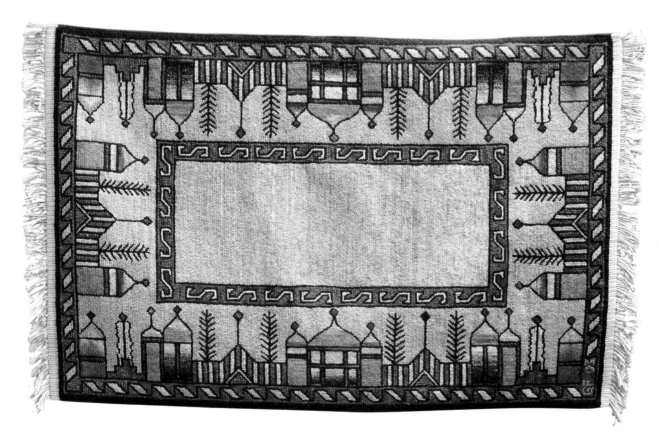

Recalling ancient tales of foreign lands, "Anatolian Borders" was named for the western plateaus of Turkey. The continuous border panel of mosque-like structures makes this rug a pleasure to view from any angle. Designed by Jane McGown Flynn. House of Price / Charco pattern. Hooked by Gail Finlayson. Ontario, Canada. 2003. 23" x 36". *Courtesy of Gail Finlayson.*

A very close cousin to traditional rug hooking, the centuries old technique of prodding or pulling short lengths of fabric through a woven base has become popular with hooking artists. "I wanted to emphasize the proddy effect by raising the bird's feathers to sit out 2 1/2" from the swampy background. To do this, I used a variety of hooked stitch heights beneath the feathers. These feathers were cut from trousers so they would fray slightly to give the feathery effect. I thought I heard the frogs croaking while I worked on this piece!" "Aquatic Hunter" was hooked using hand-cut recycled woolen and synthetic fabrics, and yarns. Designed and hooked by Lynn Franke. Ontario, Canada. 2004. 14.5" x 23". *Courtesy of Lynn Franke.*

Crewel embroidery designs are often adapted for hooked rug patterns. This fine example includes imaginary flowers, foliage, and an owl and tiny squirrel. Designed by Joan Moshimer. W. Cushing and Company. Hooked by Colleen Gervais. Ontario, Canada. 2001. 40" x 54.5". *Courtesy of Colleen Gervais.*

Having never hooked before, Gunda Gamble took a beginner's rug making course in November of 2004. Inspired by the rugs she saw and a dye class she took, "I bought some linen (to draw a pattern on) and four dyes. On the way home, I thought of the 'Fence Post' idea. The next day I took my camera and started taking pictures of the fence posts in the neighborhood, bought some natural (colored) wool, tried dyeing, and finished the project in April 2005." Designed and hooked by Gunda Gamble. Ontario, Canada. 2005. 72" x 36". *Courtesy of Gunda Gamble.*

"In 1930, Miss 'Amy Johnson' flew all alone from the south of England to Australia. Her aircraft was a second hand de Haviland Moth. Like that other great aviatrix, Amelia Earhart, she captured the imagination of the public—including my grandmother in her Manchester slum, for whom Amy Johnson was a heroine. I lived for a few years in Australia and have used colours and images of Aboriginal desert landscapes. The lands are seen from above by the aviator and the Aboriginal people. The two words have several meanings: 'attitude' because these heroines were women with attitude; and the position of an aircraft in the sky is its 'altitude.' Altitude speaks for itself, and also refers to lofty heroism. I have included recycled 'patchy' materials to reflect the repairs to the wings that Amy did herself. Her dogged look may have something to do with her leaning out of the cockpit to vomit when overcome by the engine fumes." Designed and hooked by Tanya Graham. British Columbia, Canada. 2003. 23" x 32". *Courtesy of Tanya Graham.*

Detail of "Amy Johnson." *Courtesy of Tanya Graham.*

"Josef Albers, the colour theorist, taught at the Black Mountain College in North Carolina during the 1930s. He had a huge influence on the younger generation of American painters. His sequence of paintings, 'Homage to the Square,' influenced me too, because I was intrigued by the colour BLUE. Struggling with BLUE, I was at the same time struggling with a rural life. I am a city slicker by nature. My goats proved much more intelligent than me. But in spite of these goats, I had some success in growing artichokes. I really wanted a donkey." "Artichoke Folk." Designed and hooked by Tanya Graham. British Columbia, Canada. 2006. 35" x 35". *Courtesy of Tanya Graham.*

Details of "Artichoke Folk."
Courtesy of Tanya Graham.

"Blackpool (England) is my birthplace, and is a sea-side resort for working people. I was eight years old when my father, younger sister, and I set out to see the illuminations on the promenade. We went on a double-decker bus of the old kind and took with us Timmy, our mongrel dog. As the bus slowed down for a stop, Timmy jumped off and was crushed under the back wheel. He died in my father's arms. Fifty years in, I was recovered enough to hook this mat. The thin anxious child is me; but this time Timmy is in front of the tram and escapes. The people in the shelter are holiday-makers awakened from their stupor by the activity in front of them. "Blackpool Scene." Designed and hooked by Tanya Graham. British Columbia, Canada. 2002. 21" x 22". *Courtesy of Tanya Graham.*

Detail of "Blackpool Scene." *Courtesy of Tanya Graham.*

The woolen fabric used to hook "Sweden" was hand-dyed to match the artist's living room décor. Rittermere-Hurst-Field pattern. Hooked by Sylvia Lewis. Ontario, Canada. 2003. 33" x 55". *Courtesy of Sylvia Lewis.*

Finely shaded acanthus leaf scrollwork complements an entranceway greeting. "Scroll Welcome." Designed by Jane Mc-Gown Flynn. Hooked by Dianne May. Ontario, Canada. 2004. 24"x 43". *Courtesy of Dianne May.*

"Hydrangeas" break free from a center field and spill onto a lattice work border. Subtle shading creates life-like blooms and leaves. Designed by Jane McGown Flynn. House of Price / Charco pattern. Hooked by Dianne May. Ontario, Canada. 2003. 27" x 40". *Courtesy of Dianne May.*

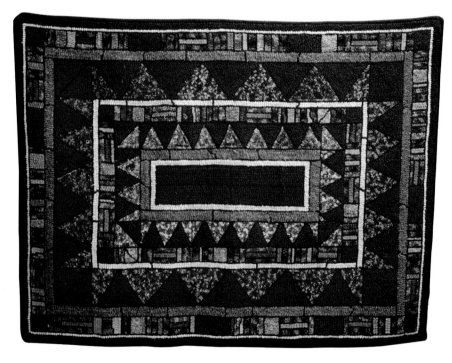

"Mosaic" was adapted from a photographed section of Roman pavement. Designed and hooked by Anne Moorhead. Ontario, Canada. 2004. 30.5" x 40.5". *Courtesy of Anne Moorhead.*

The popular designs of William Morris are showcased in "Chrysanthemums and Leaves." Rittermere-Hurst-Field pattern. Hooked by Cheronne Morris. Ontario, Canada. 2005. 41" x 18". *Courtesy of Cheronne Morris.*

Designed for the hooking artist's six and eight year old boys, "Reach for the Sky" and "Dream a New Dream" were crafted using both traditional and prodded styles of hooking. Added knitted lengths of metallic yarn "give the midnight sky some sparkle." Designed and hooked by Cheronne Morris. Ontario, Canada. 2003. Both are 28" x 34". *Courtesy of Cheronne Morris.*

Hooked for a niece and her husband to celebrate and commemorate their wedding day. Lush floral sprays, complete with shamrocks and gold-toned scrolls, surround Gillian and Paul-Francis and the date they will remember "Forever." Rittermere-Hurst-Field pattern. Hooked by Gail Nixon. Ontario, Canada. 2005. 30" x 40". *Courtesy of Gail Nixon.*

To celebrate a 30th wedding anniversary, Gail Nixon presented her sister and brother-in-law with a hooked remembrance. "Anniversary Rug." Eaton's pattern. Hooked by Gail Nixon. Ontario, Canada. 2001. 23.5" x 38.5". *Courtesy of Gail Nixon.*

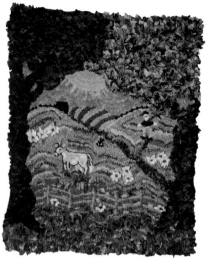

"Nixon Farm." "I hooked this rug for my parents' 50th anniversary. It is our family farm in Norval, Ontario, Canada. It holds all the things I loved about my childhood: Jersey cows, our three ponies, the apple orchard and picking apples up on the ladder, our hundred of bunnies, cats, dogs, squirrels, birds, bees, the lane to the back of the barn, lots of trees, the family swing, Mom's flower gardens and vegetable garden, the scarecrow, the pond, the ducks, our family house and barn, and of course the clothes line always full of clothes with six girls and one boy." Designed and hooked by Gail Nixon. Ontario, Canada. 1999. 36.5" x 47". *Courtesy of Gail Nixon.*

After the artist made a series of commemorative rugs for others, "It's a Cow" was "hooked for myself" using a variety of hooking techniques, including sculpting and prodding. Designed and hooked by Gail Nixon. Ontario, Canada. 2003. 32" x 26". *Courtesy of Gail Nixon.*

Sprays of "Poppies" fill a rich dark field. Flowers, buds, and leaves were skillfully hooked to appear as if speckled by sunlight. Heirloom Rugs pattern. Hooked by Sylvia Schenk. Ontario, Canada. 2002. 26" x 42". *Courtesy of Sylvia Schenk.*

Honoring the master of stained glass. "Tiffany Peacock." Designed by Jane McGown Flynn. House of Price / Charco pattern. Hooked by Sylvia Schenk. Ontario, Canada. 2001. 41" x 16". *Courtesy of Sylvia Schenk.*

In the United States, hooked images of "Scottie" dogs became popular after the public was introduced to President Roosevelt's terrier, Fala. Our neighbors to the north also embraced the furry little fellows, and Scottish terriers are often portrayed on Canadian hooked rugs. Pattern maker unknown. Hooked by Sylvia Schenk. Ontario, Canada. 2004. 24" x 37". *Courtesy of Sylvia Schenk.*

"Hydrangeas." A dark background creates depth and accentuates multi-flowered blossoms. Designed by Jane McGown Flynn. House of Price / Charco pattern. Hooked by Sylvia Schenk. Ontario, Canada. 2005. 27.5" x 43". *Courtesy of Sylvia Schenk.*

"Bear Band," a rug to delight any child, marks a special date. Rittermere-Hurst-Field pattern. Hooked by Sylvia Schenk. Ontario, Canada. 2000. 27" x 40". *Courtesy of Sylvia Schenk.*

"Not all beauty is immediately evident. Sometimes we have to look for what is not immediately apparent—and we can be rewarded by the discovery." Looking beyond the "Camouflage," we spy an exotic bird. Designed and hooked by Fannie Sinclair. Ontario, Canada. 2000. 14" x 33". *Courtesy of Fannie Sinclair.*

"Absent Friends" pays tribute to beloved rug hookers who have passed on. From left to right: Betty Dewar, Joan Moshimer, Jean Welbourn, and Margaret Rowan. Golden rings of friendship and forget-me-nots frame the unforgettable foursome, three of which wear nylon stockings. Designed and hooked by Fannie Sinclair. Ontario, Canada. 2002. 18" x 14". *Courtesy of Fannie Sinclair.*

A series of ornate borders surround "Soumac Medallion." The woolen fabric used to hook this rug's background field was hand-dyed to mimic the color changes found in woven carpets. Designed by Jane McGown Flynn. House of Price / Charco pattern. Hooked by Catharine Turner. Ontario, Canada. 2004. 30" x 38". *Courtesy of Catharine Turner.*

A personalized hooked monogram. "Celtic B" for Bernice. Designed by David Rankine. Rittermere-Hurst-Field pattern. Hooked by Bernice Wilson. Ontario, Canada. 2005. 24" x 19". *Courtesy of Bernice Wilson.*

Using subtle color changes and fine shading, "Autumn Leaves" records a favorite time of the year. Designed and hooked by Bernice Wilson. Ontario, Canada. 2005. 31" x 50". *Courtesy of Bernice Wilson.*

"Over the Rainbow." "I changed the design of this rug slightly by adding a tree and moving the clouds about. I chose bright cheerful colours because I love 'colours of cheer.'" Designed by Ingrid Hieronimus. Hooked by Charlene Wood. Ontario, Canada. 2001. 20.5" x 43". *Courtesy of Charlene Wood.*

Margaret Arraj MacDonald – Leeds, Massachusetts

Through the medium of rug hooking, Margaret Arraj MacDonald can transport you to exotic and mystical lands, seat you in the drawing room of an English manor, or bring back memories of the quilt on your beloved grandmother's bed. Inspired by such things as bits of fabric and carpet and wallpaper designs, Margaret works exclusively with woolen yarns. Her hooked works of art create a sense of peace, tranquility, and well being.

Ottoman embroidery on an eighteenth century bath wrap border was the inspiration for "Turkish Delight." Many hand-dyed woolen yarns were used to hook this lively, centuries old pattern. Hooked by Margaret Arraj MacDonald. Massachusetts. 2005. 49" x 32". *Courtesy of Margaret Arraj MacDonald.*

Motifs from two nineteenth century Chinese carpets meld. "Chinese Carpet." Hooked by Margaret Arraj MacDonald. Massachusetts. 2005. 33" x 50". *Courtesy of Margaret Arraj MacDonald.*

Symbols of immortality, "Korean Cranes" each hold a piece of polloch'o, the plant of eternal youth. Adapted from a rank badge 1848-1888 (late Choson dynasty). From the collection found in the Victoria and Albert Museum, England. Hooked by Margaret Arraj MacDonald. Massachusetts. 2004. 37" x 35". *Courtesy of Margaret Arraj MacDonald.*

Paying tribute to an antique quilt, "Crazy Fans" recalls home and family. We are reminded that the familiar is as visually exciting and spiritually rewarding as the exotic. Adapted from a circa 1880 quilt. Hooked by Margaret Arraj MacDonald. Massachusetts. 2006. 31" x 49". *Courtesy of Margaret Arraj MacDonald.*

"Persian Peace Garden" evokes a sense of spiritual tranquility through the use of design and color. Adapted from a seventeenth century Iranian prayer cloth. Hooked by Margaret Arraj MacDonald. Massachusetts. 2003. 46" x 32". *Courtesy of Margaret Arraj MacDonald.*

Simplistic "Medieval Foliage" reaches toward a striated sky. Adapted from a portion of a fifteenth century Devonshire tapestry entitled: "The Boar and the Bear Hunt." Hooked by Margaret Arraj MacDonald. Massachusetts. 2006. 24" x 70". *Courtesy of Margaret Arraj MacDonald.*

Fabric, used to fashion a nineteenth century Buddhist priest's mantle, featured a repetitive pattern that inspired "Japanese Grapes." Hooked by Margaret Arraj MacDonald. Massachusetts. 2004. 31" x 42". *Courtesy of Margaret Arraj MacDonald.*

Inspired by an appliquéd table linen from the Arts and Crafts era, "Ann Arbor Fruits" offers colorful stylized produce. Hooked by Margaret Arraj MacDonald. Massachusetts. 2004. 25" x 47". *Courtesy of Margaret Arraj MacDonald.*

Background colors illuminate the decorative elements of "Hammersmith." This hooked rug was adapted from one of a series of decorative carpets that English artist William Morris had woven in the late nineteenth century while living at Kelmscott Manor on the River Thames in Hammersmith, West London. Hooked by Margaret Arraj MacDonald. Massachusetts. 2006. 57" x 30". *Courtesy of Margaret Arraj MacDonald.*

"Turkish Flowers" spring forth from vines of a delicate nature. Hooked by Margaret Arraj MacDonald. Massachusetts. 2005. 24" x 18". *Courtesy of Margaret Arraj MacDonald.*

Outstretched limbs offer a fruit laden sanctuary for birds. With permission, Margaret Arraj MacDonald incorporated motifs from Fayek Nicolas' 1958 woven tapestry into her own hooked "Egyptian Tree." From the collection of the Ramses Wissa Wassef Art Centre. Giza, Egypt. Hooked by Margaret Arraj MacDonald. Massachusetts. 2005. 30" x 68". *Courtesy of Margaret Arraj MacDonald.*

"Water Lilies," fashioned in an Art Nouveau manner, whisper of a still pond and quiet times. Hooked by Margaret Arraj MacDonald. Massachusetts. 2005. 40" x 30". *Courtesy of Margaret Arraj MacDonald.*

Inspired by an Indian dhurrie hand-woven by inmates of Ahmenabad Prison during the turn of the last century, Margaret Arraj MacDonald hooked "Mango Prison Rug." True to the original carpet, she designed this rug to include a stylized mango vine and added an "inner border to symbolize and honor these prisoners. In such an inhuman environment, prisoners must have felt some sense of peace while weaving." Hooked by Margaret Arraj MacDonald. Massachusetts. 2005. 51" x 35". *Courtesy of Margaret Arraj MacDonald.*

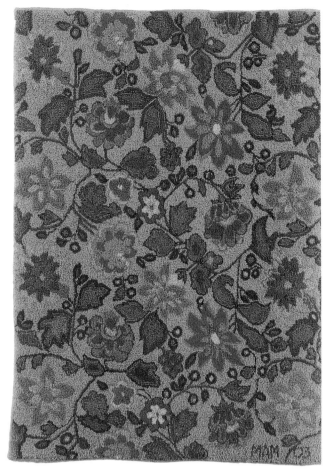

An English block print of Indian influence comes to life with hook and palette of colorful woolen yarns. "India Flora." Hooked by Margaret Arraj MacDonald. Massachusetts. 2003. 42" x 31". *Courtesy of Margaret Arraj MacDonald.*

"Japanese Chrysanthemums," hooked of many hand-dyed woolen yarns, glow like floral fireworks. Adapted from *Designs and Patterns from Historic Ornament* by W. and G. Audsley. Hooked by Margaret Arraj Mac-Donald. Massachusetts. 2002. 48" x 33". *Courtesy of Margaret Arraj MacDonald.*

Overflowing with an abundance of botanical wonders, "The English Vase" was hooked using woolen yarns of true historic color. Adapted from a mid-eighteenth century English embroidered pole screen. From the collection of the Metropolitan Museum of Art, New York. Hooked by Margaret Arraj MacDonald. Massachusetts. 2003. 38" x 31". *Courtesy of Margaret Arraj MacDonald.*

Sinuous lines and foliated forms were typical of late nineteenth century Art Nouveau designs. "Isis" was adapted from wallpaper of that era and named for an Egyptian nature goddess. Designed by C. F. A. Voysey. Hooked by Margaret Arraj MacDonald. Massachusetts. 2003. 28" x 45". *Courtesy of Margaret Arraj MacDonald.*

Decorative vines with jewel-like flowers complement a "Persian Prayer Rug." Adapted from a seventeenth century Isfahan (Iran) embroidery design. Hooked by Margaret Arraj MacDonald. Massachusetts. 2003. 46" x 32". *Courtesy of Margaret Arraj MacDonald.*

"Tibetan Rug" displays traditional peony and cloud designs. Hooked by Margaret Arraj MacDonald. Massachusetts. 2001. 49" x 31". *Courtesy of Margaret Arraj MacDonald.*

Being stylish never goes out of fashion. "Turkish Trousers" pays homage to a fragment of cloth from a pair of women's eighteenth century silk embroidered pantaloons. Hooked by Margaret Arraj MacDonald. Massachusetts. 45" x 29". *Courtesy of Margaret Arraj MacDonald.*

"Winter To Spring" was adapted from William Morris' "Jasmine" design. Hooked by Margaret Arraj MacDonald. Massachusetts. 2003. 45" x 31". *Courtesy of Margaret Arraj MacDonald.*

Inspired by embroidery from the Isle of Skros, "Greek Cockerel" is a popular symbol representing an "anarchic spirit." Hooked by Margaret Arraj MacDonald. Massachusetts. 2003. 28" x 36". *Courtesy of Margaret Arraj MacDonald.*

Hooked Advertising Art –
Past and Present

Sought after by many for its aesthetic appeal, vintage advertising art has inspired some rug hookers to pick up their hooks and wool strips and recreate likenesses of the images they admire.

Lynne Moseman's husband, Roy, admires vintage advertising art and country store memorabilia. "American Biscuit Parrot" was adapted from a sign in his collection. Hooked by Lynne Moseman. Georgia. 2003. 20" x 41". *Courtesy of Lynne Moseman.*

An all-American farm boy beckons you to try "Quinlan's Butter Sticks." A pretzel tin in Karen Detrick's vintage advertising art collection was inspiration for her hooked "Pretzel Boy." Jacqueline Designs pattern. Hooked by Karen Detrick. Ohio. 2004. 23" x 30". *Courtesy of Karen Detrick.*

Having a father who worked at John Deere's corporate office in Moline, Illinois, Liz Marino grew up around tractors. She married a farm machinery enthusiast. Wanting to make a rug for her tractor collecting husband, she contacted Neil Dahlstrom, Reference Archivist for John Deere, and was given permission to hook a reproduction of an advertisement marking the company's 75th year in business. Crafting the rug on the 200th anniversary of the birth of the company's founder, Liz dedicated her work to "Celebrating 200 Years of Progress" and "the development of America as a great farm nation." Hooked by Liz Marino. Massachusetts. 2005. 37" x 24". *Courtesy of Liz Marino, Neil Dahlstrom, and John Deere.*

Old Judge, purveyors of spices, mustard, and coffee, also offered customers decorative kitchen art. Adapted from a coffee tin in Karen Detrick's collection. "Old Judge Owl Tin." Jacqueline Designs pattern. Hooked by Karen Detrick. Ohio. 2000. 26" x 32". *Courtesy of Karen Detrick.*

The girl of every man's dreams wears "Dream Girl" hosiery. Art Deco advertising art at its best. Fashioned after a 1920s hosiery box. Hooked by Joanne Thomason. Iowa. 2004. 34" x 26". *Courtesy of Joanne Thomason.*

Karen Detrick found a vintage hosiery box complete with three pairs of the original stockings. Inspired by thoughts of warm and stylish feet, she hooked the Paramount Knitting Company's whimsical mascot. "Bear Brand Socks." Jacqueline Designs pattern. Hooked by Karen Detrick. Ohio. 2003. 21" x 28". *Courtesy of Karen Detrick.*

Over a century ago, a likeness of this tavern sign welcomed thirsty visitors to the "Kate and Leopold." The hooked reproduction now graces a twenty-first century home. Designed and hooked by Beverly Goodrich. Georgia. 2001. 38" x 42". *Courtesy of Beverly Goodrich.*

What better way to advertise yourself as a hooking artist or supplier of hooked rug equipment than with a business card showcasing the art you've hooked.

Karen Guffey, co-owner of The Dye Store, hooked "Dye Masters at their dye pots!" as an advertisement for her rug hooking business. Karen, wearing her favorite "birks" (sandals) and partner Cindy Hartman labor over boiling cauldrons, while newly dyed woolen fabric is hung to dry in the Iowa sun. Designed and hooked by Karen Guffey. Iowa. 2004. 34" x 48". *Courtesy of Karen Guffey.*

"I began 'Design in Mind' as a doodle and it grew into a self portrait that shows how ideas come to me as I hook. This is now my business card logo." Designed and hooked by Rae Reynolds Harrell. Vermont. 2002. 35" x 24". *Courtesy of Rae Reynolds Harrell.*

Destinations – Roslyn Logsdon

Maryland artist Roslyn Logsdon continues to delight us with hooked vignettes of people and places. Whether showcasing the United States or a European tour, her work invites viewers to share in the details of architecture and landscapes, and captured moments that often go unnoticed.

Using a subtly changing palette of woolen fabric strips cut 3/32" wide, artist Roslyn Logsdon hooked the ancient stones of Scotland's "Melrose Abbey." Merging structures, though solid in form, create a feeling of movement. Designed and hooked by Roslyn Logsdon. Maryland. 2004. 28" x 22". *Courtesy of Roslyn Logsdon.*

The somberness of stone gives way to a glimpse inside the "Abbey Gate." Melrose Abbey, Scotland. Designed and hooked by Roslyn Logsdon. Maryland. 2004. 22" x 21". *Courtesy of Roslyn Logsdon.*

Where does the "Cortona" stairway lead to? The look of centuries old Italian stone and mortar is achieved by hooking with a variety of tweeds. Cutting the roughly woven woolen fabric into 3/32" wide strips and then hooking with it demands skill and patience. Designed and hooked by Roslyn Logsdon. Maryland. 2002. 25" x 17". *Courtesy of Roslyn Logsdon.*

A ceiling view of England's "York Minster" offers a kaleidoscope-like image. When it comes to hooking detail within the confines of a limited space, Roslyn Logsdon is a master. Designed and hooked by Roslyn Logsdon. Maryland. 2003. 26.5" x 26". *Courtesy of Roslyn Logsdon.*

"Enchanted April" was inspired by a Tuscan garden and the book of the same name. Designed and hooked by Roslyn Logsdon. Maryland. 2003. 32.5" x 22". *Courtesy of Roslyn Logsdon.*

An architectural study of a special "Passageway" in Italy. Designed and hooked by Roslyn Logsdon. Maryland. 2003. 26" x 17". *Courtesy of Roslyn Logsdon.*

Light and shadow play on "Quiet Street Arches" in Italy. Designed and hooked by Roslyn Logsdon. Maryland. 2003. 21" x 14". *Courtesy of Roslyn Logsdon.*

Good friends, a glass of wine, and people-watching at the café—a captured moment. "Three French Women." Inspired by a number of photos and sketches. Designed and hooked by Roslyn Logsdon. Maryland. 2004. 18.5" x 19.5". *Courtesy of Roslyn Logsdon.*

Travel under the arches and follow the cobblestone road. "Corde." France. Designed and hooked by Roslyn Logsdon. Maryland. 2003. 29" x 16". *Courtesy of Roslyn Logsdon.*

"Three French Women II" is another interpretation of the aforementioned hooked vignette, this time "using a bright stash of wool." Designed and hooked by Roslyn Logsdon. Maryland. 2004. 17.5" x 19". *Courtesy of Roslyn Logsdon.*

A French sidewalk café where an exciting time was not had by all. "Rivoire." Designed and hooked by Roslyn Logsdon. Maryland. 2003. 23" x 17". *Courtesy of Roslyn Logsdon.*

"Reflections," on a glass façade building in Charlotte, North Carolina, form distorted images that are intricate and interesting. Designed and hooked by Roslyn Logsdon. Maryland. 2004. 27" x 17.5". *Courtesy of Roslyn Logsdon.*

Smile for the camera. Preserving the past with a hooked "photograph" of a 1940s family "Picnic" at Prospect Park in Brooklyn, New York. Designed and hooked by Roslyn Logsdon. Maryland. 2003. 20" x 25". *Courtesy of Roslyn Logsdon.*

Known for its cast-iron façade buildings, trendy art galleries, and close proximity to the Great White Way, Roslyn Logsdon, with hook in hand, tours New York City's "Soho, Broadway." Designed and hooked by Roslyn Logsdon. Maryland. 2004. 16" x 22". *Courtesy of Roslyn Logsdon.*

"Three Women and One Dog." Backsides immortalized; a captured moment in Damariscotta, Maine. Designed and hooked by Roslyn Logsdon. Maryland. 2004. 19" x 24". *Courtesy of Roslyn Logsdon.*

Bed Ruggs, Samplers, and Crewel – Hooked Look-A-Likes

Mimicking women's handwork of an earlier time, rug hookers replicate centuries old yarn sewn bed ruggs, needlework samplers, and embroidered crewel work.

"I collect early American antiques and 'Thankful's Bed Rugg' seemed to be the perfect addition for an old feather bed." Designed by Edyth O'Neill. Woolley Fox pattern. Hooked by Tricia Travis. Texas. 2004. 9' 10" x 8' 2". *Courtesy of Tricia Travis.*

Originally intended for use on a bed, some bed ruggs were put on the floor. "Jericho" was inspired by an 1805 yarn sewn bed rugg in Dearborn, Michigan's historic Greenfield Village. "Hooking 'Jericho' was like a good book. Once I started it I couldn't lay it down." Quail Hill Designs pattern. Hooked by June Mikoryak. Michigan. 2006. 6' 8" x 8'. *Courtesy of June Mikoryak.*

After studying the needlework motifs on early bed coverings, hooking artist Joyce Krueger designed "Ense's Bed Rugg." The woolen fabrics she hooked with were hand-dyed to give an aged "sepia" appearance. Designed by Joyce Krueger. House of Price / Primco pattern. Hooked by Joyce Krueger. Wisconsin. 2005. 55" x 44". *Courtesy of Joyce Krueger.*

Needlework samplers served as an example of skill. Barbara Ahlbrand's hooked "Sampler" pays tribute to her talents and a centuries old tradition. Hand-dyed woolen fabrics were used. Designed by Nola Heidbreder. Cactus Needle pattern. Hooked by Barbara Ahlbrand. Illinois. 2003. 30" x 32". *Courtesy of Barbara Ahlbrand.*

Lively red folk art flowers and buds enhance "Bed Rugg Fantasy." Designed by Marie Azzaro. Yankee Peddler pattern. Hooked by Lee Abrego. New Hampshire. 2002. 50" x 40". *Courtesy of Lee Abrego.*

"My mother owns quite a few antique samplers. My sister (Linda Pietz) and I grew up around these. I'm sure this influenced both of us to want to do samplers in rugs." "Floral Sampler." Designed by Linda Pietz. Cactus Needle pattern. Hooked by Nola Heidbreder. Missouri. 2002. 22" x 29". *Courtesy of Nola Heidbreder.*

Crewel work embroidery was developed in the seventeenth century during the reign of Queen Elizabeth I. Contemporary rug hookers admire the fanciful motifs and hook their own versions of the twisted woolen yarn needlework. By using gradation swatches of many values, fine shading is achieved. "Devonshire." Designed by Jane McGown Flynn. House of Price / Charco pattern. Hooked by Suzanne S. Hamer. Illinois. 1997. 21" x 27". *Courtesy of Suzanne S. Hamer.*

Choosing colors to coordinate with her bedroom décor, Betty Evans hooked "Queen Anne's Oval," a crewel design fit for royal feet. Designed by Joan Moshimer. W. Cushing and Company pattern. Hooked by Betty C. Evans. Maine. 2000. 36" x 60". *Courtesy of Betty C. Evans.*

A decorative crewel-inspired stalk, laden with fanciful motifs, reaches for the sun. "Crewel Panel." Designed by Jane Olson. Hooked by Susan Andreson. California. 2003. 30" x 18". *Courtesy of Susan Andreson.*

"Arundel Crewel," hooked with shades of blue, is enhanced by complementary additions of subdued color. Designed by Joan Moshimer. W. Cushing and Company pattern. Hooked by Betty C. Evans. Maine. 2003. 25.5" x 41.5". *Courtesy of Betty C. Evans.*

"Creative Crewel" boasts a trio of fanciful blossoms framed by stylized flowers and half diamond motifs. Directional hooking was used to "create a crewel stitch effect." Designed by Patsy Becker. Hooked by Joyce Krueger. Wisconsin. 2000. 36" x 72". *Courtesy of Joyce Krueger.*

Gene Shepherd –
Anaheim, California

Husband, father, grandfather, and Senior Pastor of Anaheim Christian Church, Gene Shepherd hooks award winning rugs, does commissioned work for private collectors, conducts weekly rug hooking classes (with an occasional teaching jaunt to Moscow), designs and sells rug hooking patterns, and undertakes writing assignments and advisory positions for the Association of Traditional Hooking Artists…all in his spare time.

"As a dedicated antique collector, I was aware of hooked rugs, but unaware the art form was still being practiced. After collecting a few old rugs, I was captivated by their appeal and decided this was something I had to try. Using craft store burlap, a crochet hook, hand-cut wool, and my wife's quilting frames, I hooked my first rug (31" x 45") in three weeks. While visiting craft stores in search of someone who knew how to finish the rug, I discovered that rug hookers met regularly in my area and had a special workshop in two weeks. My first meeting with the San Luis Obispo, California Rug Hookers in March 1998 also introduced me to Jane Olson (California's first lady of rug hooking). All these artists continue to be an influence in my life and art."

California hooking artist Gene Shepherd at work. Each time he finishes a hooking project, leftovers are set aside and used to hook "Cat's Paw," an on going endeavor. 2004. *Courtesy of Gene R. Shepherd.*

"When I moved to Anaheim, I had to give up my outdoor aviary, where I raised parakeets. Although I would often let my flock grow to as many as fifty birds at a time, I always had a special place in my heart for my original breeding stock. I made this rug to make a permanent record of these favorites. To make the pattern, I took photos of my birds, enlarged them, and then pasted together the design." "Gene's Birds." Designed and hooked by Gene R. Shepherd. California. 1999. 24" x 41.5". *Private Collection.*

"I had been looking for an excuse to experiment with cut size, color, and perspective. Inspired by the work of Gustav Klimt, I knew I wanted to use strong geometric lines in a whimsical pastoral setting. Then, while discussing a possible commission piece for an art collector who liked birch trees, I decided the time had come. Several trips to Russia have permanently seared the magical landscape of that magnificent country in my mind. It is the sort of place where the rigid lines of life intersect with a rich fantasy in art, music, and conversation. When in Russia, one never seems to know exactly what is going to happen next. I had always intended to do something that was, in my mind, 'Russian,' but had never seemed to find the correct moment or occasion to start." "Russian Birch." Designed and hooked by Gene R. Shepherd. California. 2003. 66" x 29.5". *Private Collection.*

"Designer and hooker Tatijanna Toshina, from Moscow, Russia, is holding 'Russian Snowflake.' I have taught rug hooking in Moscow on two occasions. Tatijanna is my best and most prolific student. She designed this piece and gave it to me when she visited California's Cambria Pines Rug Camp in 2003, as a result of the camp's scholarship program." Designed and hooked by Tatijanna Toshina, Moscow, Russia. 2003. 31" x 31". *Courtesy of Tatijanna Toshina and Gene R. Shepherd.*

"When I was a child, I often spent time at Miss Weigle's house. She always kept a hooked rug in progress—usually a geometric—on a frame in the corner of her living room. Watching her as a child triggered an interest in rug hooking that finally took hold of me three and a half decades later. This rug was named for her. 'Miss Weigle' was designed as a project for both beginner and experienced rug hookers. For me, this is a perfect scrap piece. Although some of the colors are used repeatedly, it's pretty much an affair where I used up what was laying around. If you really inspect the rug, you will see variations in the sections where it looks as though I used the exact same wool…I didn't." Designed and hooked by Gene R. Shepherd. California. 2004. 30" x 60". *Courtesy of Gene R. Shepherd.*

"As a coastal Californian, I know fog as a frequent visitor." Recalling Carl Sandburg's poem and utilizing a stash of woolen fabric "that was not quite right for the spot you intended," Gene Shepherd spent about seven months hooking "Fog." Thirteen cats, representing misty and murky conditions, pay a nighttime visit to Gene's palm-treed neighborhood. A border panel of traditional cat's paw motifs frames the whimsical play on words. Designed and hooked by Gene R. Shepherd. California. 2000. 33" x 69.5". *Private Collection.*

Each year during the first full week of June, Gene Shepherd serves as director and also teaches at the Cambria Pines Rug Camp in Cambria, California. About 120 students from all over the United States and Canada come together to spend an informative and enjoyable week sharing their love of rug hooking. "Every year I offer an evening mini class 'scrap wool' project. I am big on using found wool and leftovers." In 2003, the class topic "Legends of Rug Hooking Chair Pads" was a runaway success. Of the six variations to choose from, each with a cat's paw motif, this tribute to California's first lady of rug hooking—artist, designer, and teacher, Jane Olson—was the most popular. "Jane Olson Sat Here." Designed and hooked by Gene R. Shepherd. California. 2003. Diameter 13". *Courtesy of Gene R. Shepherd.*

"Did you ever wonder why Franklin Delano Roosevelt was the only United States President elected to four terms? While that question would raise spirited debate amongst politicians and historians, makers of traditional hand-hooked rugs should be quick to promote a theory of our own. FDR kept two hand-hooked rugs in his private retreat at Hyde Park, New York. Surely it is natural for rug hooking artists to conclude that anyone with such impeccable taste must have been destined for greatness. Indeed, one of his rugs did symbolize the pinnacle of political achievement. However, the other was equally powerful, in that it captured the endearing, approachable quality that made Roosevelt such a beloved leader. Just as we value and use hooked rugs for their beauty, warmth, and the personal statements they make, so too, did FDR. In fact, he used them in the very place where he truly felt at home."

In 2001, The United States Department of the Interior began working with a committee of interested citizens to refurbish and restore Top Cottage, FDR's Hyde Park, New York retreat. Unfortunately many items, including the hooked rugs, did not survive. With only vague black and white photographs and inventory information, Gene Shepherd was commissioned to replicate two Top Cottage hooked rugs.

Note: This author most certainly agrees with Gene Shepherd's astute commentary and can attest to FDR's fondness for hooked rugs. Stricken with polio during the summer of 1921, Roosevelt traveled to the small rural community of Warm Springs, Georgia, to partake in the warm water therapy that proved to be beneficial to those with weakened muscles. There he built a small cottage, "the Little White House," which was (and still is) decorated with hooked rugs.

In FDR's words, "I began talking about building a small place to go to 'escape the mob.'" *Courtesy of the National Park Service and the United States Department of the Interior.*

President Roosevelt and his Scottish terrier, Fala, relax at Top Cottage. Photo taken in 1944. *Courtesy of the Franklin D. Roosevelt Presidential Library and the United States Department of the Interior.*

This photo, taken in May 1945, just shortly after FDR's death, shows his Presidential Seal hooked rug in place before a Top Cottage fireplace. The formal, skillfully executed, and finely shaded 4' by 6' rectangular rug was most likely crafted by an experienced rug hooker. *Courtesy of the Franklin D. Roosevelt Library and the United States Department of the Interior.*

Thanks to Gene Shepherd's hooking talents, a replica of FDR's Presidential Seal hooked rug once again graces Top Cottage. Photo taken in 2004. *Courtesy of the National Park Service and the United States Department of the Interior.*

A likeness of FDR's terrier companion, Fala, was hooked by first grade students from the Joseph Clisby School in Macon, Georgia, and presented to the president in 1942. As shown in this May 1945 Top Cottage photo, the 28.5" round rug rests in a place of honor beneath the president's desk. Unfortunately the obscured view is all that remains of the children's gift. *Courtesy of the Franklin D. Roosevelt Library and the United States Department of the Interior.*

A closer look at Gene Shepherd's hooked reproduction of Fala. Photo taken in 2004. *Courtesy of the National Park Service and the United States Department of the Interior.*

With little to go on but an incomplete photo and brief written description, Gene Shepherd created this tribute to the first graders' hooked portrait of Fala, returning it once more to FDR's New York retreat. Photo taken in 2004. *Courtesy of the National Park Service and the United States Department of the Interior.*

Country Gatherings –
San Antonio, Texas

Should you be in the San Antonio area, do stop in at Tricia Travis' Country Gatherings. Offering instruction, hooking equipment, and a plentiful array of beautiful woolen fabrics, Country Gatherings is a place where rug hookers come together to enjoy their craft and each other's company. What a delightful way to spend the day.

Country Gatherings' wool stash offers the perfect colors and textures for all your hooking projects. 2005. *Courtesy of Country Gatherings* LLC.

Rug hooking teacher and Country Gatherings owner Tricia Travis offers helpful hints. 2005. *Courtesy of Country Gatherings* LLC.

In her spare time, Tricia Travis loves to hook rugs. Her "Woolley Fox," hooked with 8/32" wide strips of hand-dyed woolen fabric, sports keen blue eyes, a mottled fur coat, and contouring line background. Other examples of Tricia's hooked handiwork can be found elsewhere in this book. Designed by Edyth O'Neill. Woolley Fox pattern. Hooked by Tricia Travis. Texas. 2000. 30" x 42". *Courtesy of Tricia Travis.*

Pineapples, symbols of hospitality, grace Diana Harris' nearly completed hooked rug. "Pineapple Antique." Quail Hill pattern. Hooked by Diana Harris. Texas. 2005. Finished size 36.5" x 72". *Courtesy of Diana Harris.*

Shortly after the aforementioned photo was taken, Jo Hamm completed "Lady Diana." The rug was originally intended to be hooked with woolen fabric cut 3/32" or 4/32" wide, but Jo hooked the design using a wider cut, thus creating a more "antique" and primitive look. Designed by Jane McGown Flynn. House of Price / Charco pattern. Hooked by Jo Hamm. Texas. 2005. 34" x 60". *Courtesy of Jo Hamm.*

Jo Hamm proudly displays "Lady Diana," a work in progress. 2005. *Courtesy of Jo Hamm.*

As they share similar backgrounds, interests, and physical characteristics, Maxine Thomas, a contemporary folk art painter and author, designed this whimsical pattern for her newfound "twin," Georgeanne Wertheim. Seated at her hooking frame, Georgeanne works on "Juneteenth." 2005. *Courtesy of Georgeanne Wertheim.*

"Juneteeth," the finished product. Designed by Maxine Thomas. Hooked by Georgeanne Wertheim. Texas. 2005. 22.5" x 31. *Courtesy of Georgeanne Wertheim.*

Floral Designs

Whether realistic or imaginary, floral designs have always been popular with rug hookers. In the 1860s, using discarded clothing and fabrics, rug makers hooked underfoot gardens. In the 1960s, flower power thrived. And surely rug hookers will continue to create botanical wonders beyond the 2060s.

"Millbrook," a favorite of many, was featured on the cover of the ATHA March 2004 newsletter. Finely shaded ornamental scrolls and floral sprays, complete with pussy willow branches, appear to glow against a rich dark background. Jane Olson pattern. Hooked by Sharon Garland. Oregon. 2001. 66" x 38". *Courtesy of Sharon Garland and ATHA (Association of Traditional Hooking Artists).*

"English Garden," a hooked display of Mother Nature's jewel box, was skillfully crafted using the artist's own hand-dyed woolen fabrics. Designed by Pearl McGown. W. Cushing and Company pattern. Hooked by Barbara D. Pond. Vermont. 2001. 60" x 47.5". *Courtesy of Barbara D. Pond.*

"I decided to interpret this piece in the style of the seventeenth century Dutch Masters, a time when the tulip was prized and dominated the thinking of painters and gardeners. In my interpretation, the Rembrandt-style tulip is prominent, with the roses of only slightly less importance; the primroses, fern, and forget-me-nots recede into the dark and luxurious background. I also added an assortment of insects typical of the genre. I planned the color scheme to evoke the richness of the Dutch style." "Floral Potpourri." Designed by Jane McGown Flynn. House of Price / Charco pattern. Hooked by Susan Higgins, California. 1998. 26" x 20". *Courtesy of Susan Higgins*.

Details of "Floral Potpourri." *Courtesy of Susan Higgins.*

To achieve the likeness of real flowers, rug hooking artist Joyce Krueger hooked these delicate magnolias using an eleven value gradation swatch of woolen fabric cut into 3/32" wide strips. "Magnolias of Eugene." Designed by Jane McGown Flynn. House of Price / Charco pattern. Hooked by Joyce Krueger. Wisconsin. 2002. 20" x 34". *Courtesy of Joyce Krueger.*

The technique of "hoving" up, or raising the pile of a hooked rug to varying heights, is reminiscent of the deep sculptured carpets of Germany, Holland, and France. Exposure to these three dimensional rugs most likely inspired early immigrants in Waldoboro, Maine to create their own versions with hook, grain sacks, and rags. The tradition continues among contemporary rug hookers. Maine's own rug hooking artist and teacher, Jacqueline Hansen, has been instrumental in promoting and instructing many in the Waldoboro-style of rug hooking. "Waldoboro." Jacqueline Designs pattern. Hooked by Barbara Mabbs Robinson. New Hampshire. 2003. 30" x 46". *Courtesy of Barbara Mabbs Robinson.*

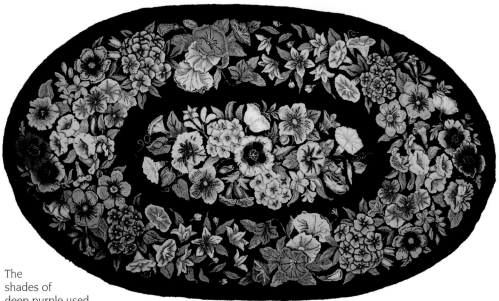

The shades of deep purple used to hook the background of "Dream Garden" complement and intensify the colors of its many flowers. Heirloom Rugs pattern. Hooked by Barbara D. Pond. Vermont. 1999. 49" x 79.5". *Courtesy of Barbara D. Pond.*

Due to the absence of true color, hooking life-like white flowers can be difficult. Suzanne Hamer accepted the challenge and skillfully hooked "Interlude." Designed by Jane McGown Flynn. House of Price / Charco pattern. Hooked by Suzanne S. Hamer. Illinois. 2001. 18" x 14.5". *Courtesy of Suzanne S. Hamer.*

Sure to produce sweet dreams, a soft pink, finely shaded "Victoria's Rose" was used to cover a dainty pillow. Designed by Victoria Hart Ingalls. Victoria Hart Ingalls pattern. Hooked by Lorraine B. Beaver. Missouri. 1998. 9.5" x 13.5". *Courtesy of Lorraine B. Beaver.*

"My Secret Garden" reveals a favorite spot of rug hooking artist and teacher Ramona Maddox. After reclaiming an overgrown area, foxglove, Ramona's favorite flower, bloomed in profusion, thanking the determined gardener with a scented and color-filled nook. Designed by Melody Hoops. Fleecewood patterns. Hooked by Ramona Maddox. Tennessee. 2003. 66" x 18". *Courtesy of Ramona Maddox.*

Finely shaded, realistic looking roses are generally hooked with a strip of woolen fabric cut 3/32" or 4/32" wide. Talented rug hooking artist Norma Flodman was able to achieve that fine shaded look by using a wider 8/32" strip. "8 Cut Rose." Jane Olson pattern. Hooked by Norma Flodman. Massachusetts and California. 2003. 36" x 36". *Courtesy of Norma Flodman.*

A delicate, finely shaded tulip trio is framed by leafy scrolls that echo many of the shades used to hook the centerpiece. "Awakening." Designed by Jane McGown Flynn. House of Price / Charco pattern. Hooked by Amy Spokes. Vermont. 1999. 36" x 41.5". *Courtesy of Amy Spokes.*

Ornate scrolls with curlicue details contain a restrained floral medallion. "Jennifer." Designed by Jane McGown Flynn. House of Price / Charco pattern. Hooked by Judy Howarth. Maine. 2002. 23" x 36". *Courtesy of Judy Howarth.*

Another interpretation of the aforementioned "Jennifer," hooked in a pastel palette. Designed by Jane McGown Flynn. House of Price / Charco pattern. Hooked by Lorraine B. Beaver. Missouri. 1995. 24" x 36". *Courtesy of Lorraine B. Beaver.*

A springtime "Floral" bouquet heralds the season of new beginnings. Note how the finely shaded tulip leaves form a star-like backdrop for the center bloom. Pattern maker unknown. Hooked by Judy Howarth. Maine. 1998. 23" x 41". *Courtesy of Judy Howarth.*

Simple daisy nosegays complement reverse image garlands. The dark background intensifies the floral colors. Name of pattern and pattern maker unknown. Hooked by Jeanne Laplante. Vermont. 2003. 37" x 71". *Courtesy of Jeanne Laplante.*

"Floral Tapestry." Twisted rope borders contain a carpet of lush flowers and foliage, a tribute to centuries old woven textiles. Prairie Craft House pattern. Hooked by Carole Beeson. Missouri. 41" x 74". *Courtesy of Carole Beeson.*

"Snuffy Tyler, a retired San Francisco architect, designed this rug of California poppies for his wife, Loyce. When I started hooking about 1994, Loyce gave me her original pattern because I admired it. I call this rug "Loyce's Poppies," since she never had given it a name." Designed by Snuffy Tyler. Hooked by Grace M. Miller. Oregon. 1997. 27" x 56". *Courtesy of Grace M. Miller.*

"For years, I have taken photos of poppies in my garden with the idea of hooking one. And why not do a giant poppy?" A cheerful checkerboard edge completes the floral portrait. Designed and hooked by Judy Fresk. Connecticut. 2003. 34" x 35.5". *Courtesy of Judy Fresk.*

Hooked with "lots of love" for a sunflower-admiring sister and her husband. Like those blowing in a summer breeze, "Sunflowers" leave the confines of the center field and toss and turn on a lively checkerboard border. Designed and hooked by Diane Yudin. Connecticut. 2000. 36" x 36". *Courtesy of Diane Yudin.*

Five vibrant blooms hooked for a special daughter. "Poppies for Mary Lou." Designed and hooked by Carolyn Barney. New Hampshire. 2002. 25" x 32". *Courtesy of Carolyn Barney.*

At rest in "My Patch" of sunflowers. The many shades of gold used to hook flower heads were also used to hooked the linear border that frames this farm-land picture postcard image. Note the mottled background sky. Jo Jules pattern. Hooked by Helen Goldsmith. Oregon. 2001. 21" x 31". *Courtesy of Helen Goldsmith.*

"Michelle's Garden." "Inspiration for this rug came from my daughter and her garden. The year I designed the pattern, she grew huge strawberries and sunflowers of many colors, which attracted a variety of birds. She is also raising two daughters, represented by the sweet peas." Designed and hooked by Sherry Jones. Massachusetts. 2001. 30" x 42". *Courtesy of Sherry Jones.*

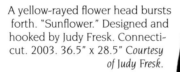

A yellow-rayed flower head bursts forth. "Sunflower." Designed and hooked by Judy Fresk. Connecticut. 2003. 36.5" x 28.5" *Courtesy of Judy Fresk.*

Like twinkling lights set upon a variegated field, lily of the valley stalks illuminate pansy trios. "Leona." Designed by Jane McGown Flynn. House of Price / Charco pattern. Hooked by Joan Watterson. Oregon. 2004. 26" x 41.5". *Courtesy of Joan Watterson.*

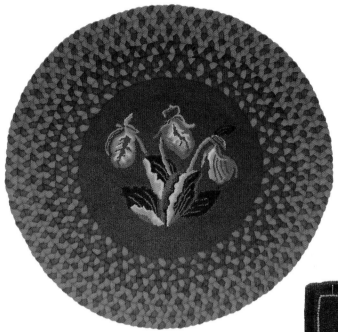

Coordinating braids complement and protect pink "Lady's Slippers." Jacqueline Designs pattern. Hooked by Anne P. Lynch. Maine. 1999. Diameter 26". *Courtesy of Anne P. Lynch.*

"'Orchids' was inspired by a series of watercolors by Brun of France. Brun was commissioned by the Parisian flower collector Emile Libreck, who was keen to have his extensive and rare orchid collection recorded for posterity. The beauty of these paintings overwhelmed me. At the same time, I was very much interested in obtaining botanical accuracy in my work. I decided upon a dendrobium since I have these in my personal collection and they capture the feeling I was looking for. I received permission to use Brun's watercolor of 'Dendrobium Nobile' as the basis for this rug. This piece was done from a palette of colors that I used as if painting. I love the richness, reality, and mystery of this piece—working toward dark, smoky, blended tones, with the orchids highlighted across the center." "Orchids." Adaptation of a watercolor by Alexandre Brun. France. 1892-94. Hooked by Susan Higgins. California. 1999. 17" x 23". *Courtesy of Susan Higgins.*

Detail of "Orchids." *Courtesy of Susan Higgins.*

"This was my very first project. My neighbor helped me get started. I dip-dyed the wool for 'Tulips' and was off on a fun new project." Woolie Delight pattern. Hooked by Judith Yokiel. Iowa. 2004. 9.5" x 9.5". *Courtesy of Judith Yokiel.*

A reminder from Chief Seattle, "Earth does not belong to us. We belong to the earth." Bees buzz above a colorful imaginary garden. "Garden II." Designed and hooked by Sally D'Albora. Maryland. 2000. 30" x 48". *Courtesy of Sally D'Albora.*

"Primitive Flowers – Under the Sea." Free floating fanciful flowers are contained by seaweed-like foliage. A small bird sits on a sea fan in the bottom right hand corner. Beverly Conway Designs pattern. Hooked by Nancy L. Taylor. Maine. 2004. 37" x 55". *Courtesy of Nancy L. Taylor.*

A primary palette of red, blue, and yellow was used to fashion "Primitive Garden Runner." Birds and butterflies join imaginary flowers. Designed by Susan Feller. Ruckman Mill Farms pattern. Hooked by June Willingham. Georgia. 2004. 26" x 72". *Courtesy of June Willingham.*

Enjoying a carefree use of color, "Pretend Flowers" branch out from a central bloom. Designed and hooked by Judy Quintman. North Carolina. 2004. 30" x 49". *Courtesy of Judy Quintman.*

Whimsical folk art flowers are contained within a scalloped edge. Bits of color fleck the neutral background. Adapted from an antique rug in the collection of the Shelburne Museum, Shelburne, Vermont. "Scalloped Edge Floral." Red Clover Rugs pattern, licensed agent of the Shelburne Museum. Hooked by Louise Royka Gleason. Massachusetts. 2005. 24" x 44". *Courtesy of Louise Royka Gleason.*

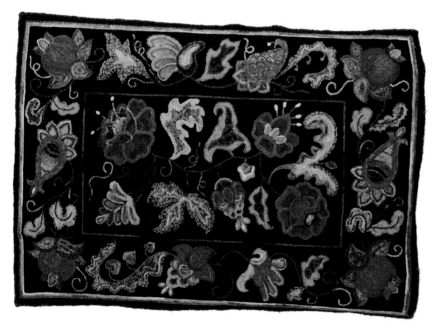

A "Rhapsody" of crewel motifs, hooked in lively "nontraditional fashion," are vibrant against a black background. "I learned that if you keep the chroma up, nothing looks 'out of place' and bright." Designed by Ramona Orihill. REO Designs pattern. Hooked by Sharon Saknit. California. 2003. 32" x 44.5". *Courtesy of Sharon Saknit.*

Detail of "Rhapsody." *Courtesy of Sharon Saknit.*

Crewel-like flowers dance on a dark field. "Antique Floral." Designed by Emma Lou Lais. Hooked by Alayne Riddle. Missouri. 1999. 30" x 48". *Courtesy of Alayne Riddle.*

"This is the third rug I ever hooked and was inspired by my husband's garden, which contains poppies, lilies, irises, nasturtiums, and peonies scattered about just as he wishes. Much of it was made of coat wool, the only wool available to me at the time. Despite its many problems, we've enjoyed it very much. It is the first of a series that I hope to hook in the next few years—each emphasizing one of the flowers shown." "Wayne's Garden." Designed and hooked by Carol Morris Petillo. Maine. 2003. 28.5" x 28.5". *Courtesy of Carol Morris Petillo.*

Concentric linear borders join a variegated background to enhance a stylized floral display. Adapted from an antique hooked rug. Hooked by Susan Andreson. California. 1996. 22" x 30". *Courtesy of Susan Andreson.*

Round rugs, charming and accommodating, are—for reasons unknown—not often hooked. This antique look-a-like, a welcome return to circular patterns, offers a simple yet charming floral and vine motif. "Old Fashion Rose." Designed and hooked by Donna Beaudoin. Vermont. 2001. Diameter 34". *Courtesy of Donna Beaudoin.*

Recalling your "Grandmother's Rug" of the 1930s and 40s. Designed by Jane McGown Flynn. House of Price / Charco pattern. Hooked by Shirley M. Dillard. Georgia. 2003. 27" x 39". *Courtesy of Shirley M. Dillard.*

"I hooked this rug the year my daughter returned home at 39 to finish college. It all worked out fine. She got two degrees and I finished the rug and we still are good friends." Folk art flowers, adapted from an old china pattern, fill a neutral field. "China Rose." Barbara Brown pattern. Hooked by Laura Phinney. Maine. 1997. 26" x 52". *Courtesy of Laura Phinney.*

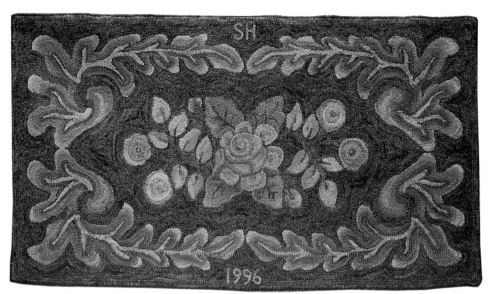

"'Little Millbury' is reminiscent of the early rugs that were crudely drawn. I love the simple flowers and the huge, almost out of proportion, leafy scroll. In this piece, I was trying to use unusual and bright colors, and carefully integrate the physical layout of the loops into the design. I wanted to experiment with luscious color that roamed through the piece and large loops." Designed by Jane McGown Flynn. House of Price / Charco pattern. Hooked by Susan Higgins. California. 1996. 24" x 43". *Courtesy of Susan Higgins.*

Crazy quilt motifs make pleasing hooked rug patterns. Adapted from an antique rug that was hooked in the Waldoboro-style (raised and clipped). "Crazy Quilt Primitive." Jacqueline Designs pattern. Hooked by Jacqueline Hansen. Maine. 2003. 40" x 23". *Courtesy of Jacqueline Hansen.*

Detail of "Little Millbury." *Courtesy of Susan Higgins.*

Inspired by Pennsylvania Dutch quilts, Betsy Gerakaris crafted "Grandmother's Quilt." Designed and hooked by Betsy Gerakaris. Connecticut. 2004. 35" x 25". *Courtesy of Betsy Gerakaris.*

"Made with love for my oldest granddaughter," and sure to become a treasured heirloom. Cheerful, imaginary flowers decorate "Michelle's Flowers." Designed and hooked by Betsy Gerakaris. Connecticut. 2001. 31" x 24". *Courtesy of Betsy Gerakaris.*

Reminiscent of vintage rugs, squiggles and flowers form a pleasing block pattern. "Floral Geometric". Designed by Barbara Brown. Hooked by Deborah Foster. Maine. 2004. 36" x 54". *Courtesy of Deborah Foster.*

A decorative window frame showcases floral quadruplets. The all over use of color makes for an aesthetically pleasing rug. "The Meadow." Jane Olson pattern. Hooked by Helen Goldsmith. Oregon. 2003. 30" x 30". *Courtesy of Helen Goldsmith.*

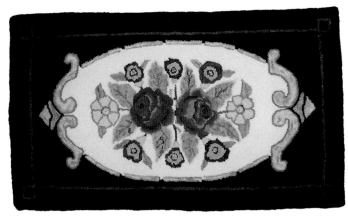

Hooked rugs with decorative tray-like center medallions were popular in the late 1800s and early 1900s. "Rose Tray." Pattern maker unknown. Most likely adapted from an early Edward Sands Frost pattern. Hooked by Doris M. Hennessy. Maine. 2001. 17" x 29". *Courtesy of Doris M. Hennessy.*

A limited use of color makes a vibrant and spirited statement. American Thread pattern. Hooked by Ruth Ann Boynton. Connecticut. 2005. 23.5" x 36.5". *Courtesy of Ruth Ann Boynton.*

"I was attempting an expressive interpretation of these flowers, taking a bold approach. I used only three main colors, intermixing freely among the floral elements. The background color to me is a most exciting and happy choice, nowhere present in the other elements and an almost tropical contrast to the pinks, reds and browns." "My Delight," a comforting place to rest one's head. Designed by Jane McGown Flynn. House of Price/ Charco pattern. Hooked by Susan Higgins. California. 1999. 14" x 18". Courtesy of Susan Higgins.

After an East Coast visit to Susan Andreson's Martha's Vineyard island home, West Coast rug hooking artist and teacher Jane Olson photographed and drew up a pattern of "Going My Way" irises. She also hand-dyed the woolen fabrics Susan used to hook this tribute to a "fine spring day." Designed by Jane Olson. Hooked by Susan Andreson. California and Massachusetts. 2000. 23" x 35". *Courtesy of Susan Andreson.*

Luminescent hooked flowers, finely shaded with strips of hand-dyed woolen fabric, are contained within a scalloped ribbon fence. "Janis Lynn." Designed by Jane Olson. Hooked by Helen Goldsmith. Oregon. 2000. 32" x 47". *Courtesy of Helen Goldsmith.*

Flowing ribbons intertwine with dainty violets protecting and complementing a delicate rose bouquet. Fine shading, used throughout the rug, gives the ribbon a realistic sheen. "Roses and Violets." Designed by Victoria Hart Ingalls. Victoria Hart Ingalls pattern. Hooked by Alayne Riddle. Missouri. 1995. 29" x 32". *Courtesy of Alayne Riddle.*

Pure and simple. "I designed this rug because of my love of 'Morning Glories.'" Open trumpets, buds, and meandering vines form a delicate grid-like design. Designed and hooked by Jane Olson. California. 1999. 30" x 40". *Courtesy of Jane Olson.*

So life-like you can almost smell the subtle scent of this exceptional "Rose." The small, finely shaded study was hooked on a homespun foundation. Designed by Margaret Hunt Masters. Prairie Craft House pattern. Hooked by Lorraine B. Beaver. Missouri. 2002. 6" x 8". *Courtesy of Lorraine B. Beaver.*

Seven roses in full bloom rest upon a mottled field. "Faye's Thimble Rose." Designed by Linda Brown. Hooked by Dorothy Rezac. Kansas. 2004. 8.5" x 23". *Courtesy of Dorothy Rezac.*

Octagonal borders frame a dozen "Floral Prints." Woolen fabric cut into strips 3/32" wide was used throughout this decorative study. Designed by Pearl McGown. W. Cushing and Company pattern. Hooked by Fay Fowler. Missouri. 1998. 54" x 95". *Courtesy of Fay Fowler.*

Niagara Falls

"When I married my husband Paul, he suggested we go to Niagara Falls for our honeymoon. I thought that was cute and corny. Upon our return, I decorated our bedroom with my vintage wedding dress and Niagara Falls souvenirs. So when I started to hook rugs, I thought I would like to do 'the Falls' at night. They are so beautiful in person at night. A friend gave me a travel brochure from the 1930s that had a great picture of what I wanted to hook. I hooked two hearts at the bottom of the Falls—my private message that I love this man." Adapted from a 1930s travel brochure and made into a pattern by Sharon Townsend. Hooked by Nola A. Heidbreder. Missouri. 1998. 49" x 33.5". *Courtesy of Nola A. Heidbreder.*

Trish Johnson –
Fergus, Ontario, Canada

"I take pictures and I hook rugs and lately I've been trying to quilt. My work is very personal. I think of it as a visual diary. I am dealing with the problems and joys of being a woman, at home with children, of becoming middle-aged, of children leaving home, of time passing and being a stranger in a strange land and now a stranger at home. What is home? Maybe we're all just passing through. I am interested in the debris of human life, the discarded toys, how people arrange their 'stuff' and the chaos of everyday life. I always start with a photograph. Some of my photographs I have chosen to hook as rugs. A photo is usually small, black and white, glossy, perfect, and the process is fast, i.e., 1/125 of a second. Much of my photographic work is about the quality of light, whereas hooking a rug is a slow process—thinking about the same image for up to a year. You have to think that it is an important image in order to invest that kind of time. This art is big, with vibrant colour. Texture is important and perfection is not. Colour intrigues me. I like a high key palette. Subtle, I am not. One of the best things about rug hooking is it feels good to do. It is a most pleasant way to while away a long winter's evening.

"I have been working on a series of rugs depicting places important to my family's history. I am fascinated by old letters and diaries and am starting to add text to my work. Maps interest me and I have started combining maps with my childhood memories. I am also working on a 'Memories of my Mother' rug.

"I like the traditional aspects of rug hooking. I think about my aunts and my grandmothers and how much needlework, sewing, quilting, and rug hooking they accomplished while raising a family. I started to hook rugs because I could do it while my babies slept. I have four children. I am continuing to work in both disciplines."

"I have a gift from my daughter, a mug from Starbucks (where she worked at the time) inscribed with 'Every Leaf a Miracle.' I'm tempted to say that I get all my sentiments from Starbucks, but of course the quote is from an earlier source, Walt Whitman. Every leaf is a miracle and it is a further miracle to create the illusion of leaves with some scrappy bits of wool and a hook. I laid some real leaves on my scanner and pushed them around until I was satisfied and printed them out. The great colour combination here is the oak leaf that has complementary violet up against a very yellow green. The ferns were dip-dyed to ending pink." Designed and hooked by Trish Johnson. Ontario, Canada. 2003. 12" x 16". *Courtesy of Trish Johnson.*

"I had hooked a smaller version of this that I called "A Gift from Suzanne to Leonard," named for the Leonard Cohen song, 'Suzanne.' My grandmother, who lived to be almost 103, always had a couple of slices of orange on the saucer of her teacup. It was one of her favorites. I hooked this version with a #8 cut (8/32") and am pleased with it. I think it has more depth. The wide cut is almost like working with a wide brush; it gives a more impressionistic effect. I think you can tell I am an admirer of van Gogh." "Tea and Oranges." Designed and hooked by Trish Johnson. Ontario, Canada. 2004. 18.5" x 19". *Courtesy of Trish Johnson.*

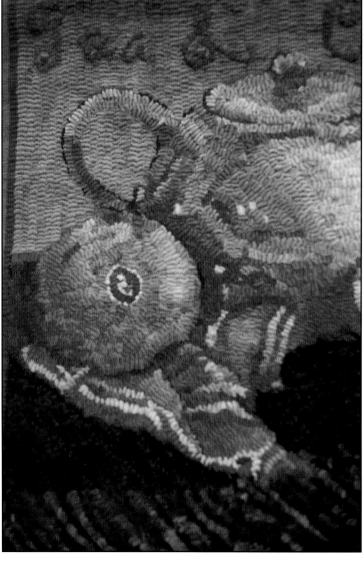

Details of "Tea and Oranges." *Courtesy of Trish Johnson.*

"I had just returned to Canada from living in California and I was lonesome for some everyday flowers. I was tired of the exotic. I based this design on a photograph of daylilies that I took in my grandmother's yard at Oak Point, New Brunswick. I was so happy to see the wild patches of daylilies that grow in abundance along the roadside, escapees from some earlier garden. "Day Lily #1" and "Day Lily #2." Designed and hooked by Trish Johnson. Ontario, Canada. 2000. 10" x 9" and 10" x 10.5". *Courtesy of Trish Johnson.*

"I hooked this for a beginner's shading course. I changed the pattern by cropping it so the rose was no longer centered and since I am not a straight line hooker, I changed the lattice work to run on the diagonal." "Blue Moon." Adapted from a design by Ingrid Hieronimus. Hooked by Trish Johnson. Ontario, Canada. 2002. 15" x 12". *Courtesy of Trish Johnson.*

"Dandelions are one of the first signs of spring, and frequently one of our first gifts to our mothers. I like dandelions. I hooked this piece in the spring of 2002, just after my husband had been diagnosed with a rare cancer that was showing up in Viet Nam veterans who had been exposed to Agent Orange. The only herbicide he has ever been exposed to is that used to rid lawns of dandelions. This dandelion is uprooted, the way I felt at the time. It has been four years and my husband is fine. The dandelion is proddy, the roots are crocheted yarn, and the seedpod is sculptured lopi wool (yarn). I hooked 'Dandelion' with a herringbone tweed background, as is and cut the same herringbone tweed on the bias to bind it." Designed and hooked by Trish Johnson. Ontario, Canada. 2002. 13.5" x 10.5". *Courtesy of Trish Johnson.*

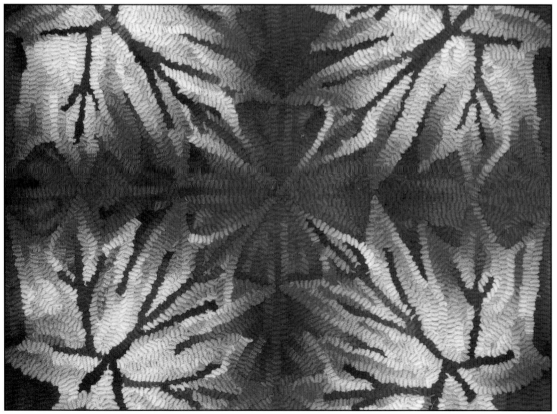

"My inspiration for 'Maple Leaf Rug' was the red sugar maples against a blue sky. I cut templates by folding squares of origami paper. It is all hooked with dip-dyed wool changing from blue to blue violet and yellow to orange. The yellow and violet are complementary, as are the sky and the orange, but the unusual combination is when the orange and the purple meet. I remember a girl in my grade nine class who wore a purple wide wale corduroy skirt with an orange poor boy sweater. I guess that made more of an impression on me than I thought." Designed and hooked by Trish Johnson. Ontario, Canada. 2004. 32" x 32". *Courtesy of Trish Johnson.*

Detail Of "Maple Leaf Rug." *Courtesy of Trish Johnson.*

"This is an old autograph verse that my Uncle Cecil wrote in my mother's autograph book and that my mother wrote in mine. It is a variation on another favorite of hers, 'to thine own self be true.' Love and canoes are joined in the Canadian psyche. Pierre Berton said, 'A Canadian is someone who knows how to make love in a canoe.' The image is of my son Douglas, age about 17, at Camp Pinecrest in the Muskokas. My children have spent most of the summers of their lives at camp jumping off high rocks into clear water. One of the hardest parts of being a mother is letting your children go, to camp or out in a canoe. Douglas has recently left home for university. He really is paddling his own canoe now. I chose an Arts and Crafts movement typeface and a border evocative of native quillwork." "Love Many Trust Few or Advice From Your Mother." Designed and hooked by Trish Johnson. Ontario, Canada. 2003. 13" x 13". *Courtesy of Trish Johnson.*

Detail of "Love Many Trust Few Or Advice From Your Mother." *Courtesy of Trish Johnson.*

"I hooked 'Culley's Cottage' because I was teaching a workshop on making changes to commercial patterns. I was part of a teaching team, so we each hooked a different season. Hooking a commercial pattern is not my usual modus operandi. I found that I needed visual references, so I shot photos to match the pattern: one of the house down the street, one of my neighbor Roger's fireplace, the evergreen is Collin's next door, the deciduous tree is Mrs. Loney's, but the child is mine. I added my son Patrick shoveling snow. That made the piece my own." George Culley Collection. Rittermere-Hurst-Field pattern. Hooked by Trish Johnson. Ontario, Canada, 2004. 24.5" x 30.5". *Courtesy of Trish Johnson*.

Detail Of "Culley's Cottage.
Courtesy of Trish Johnson.

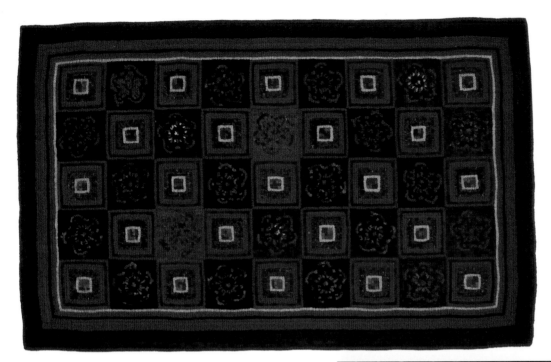

"Geometric or Old Hippies Never Die." "I started this geometric to give myself a break from hooking pictorials. I thought it would be easy. Of course nothing ever is. The colour choice was too wide open, anything could be any colour, so I spent a lot of time changing my mind and changing the colours. When I started out, I was going to alternate hit or miss squares with a simple flower motif but it soon took off on its own. It is reminiscent of a pair of Afghani embroidered boots I had in the 60s." Designed and hooked by Trish Johnson. Ontario, Canada. 2004. 32" x51". *Courtesy of Trish Johnson.*

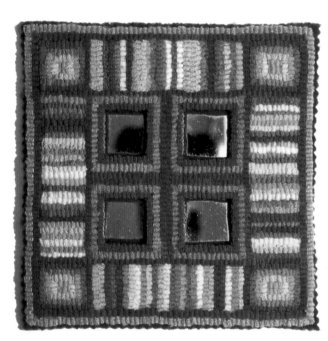

"Quartet Mirror Tile." "This is a small piece and good for using up leftover partial swatches. It is hit and miss and reminds me of brightly coloured beach towels. I thought it would make a nice gift for a young person and intended to give it to my daughter but so far I have kept it. Designed by Helen Barrett. Hooked by Trish Johnson. Ontario, Canada. 2002. 7" x 7". *Courtesy of Trish Johnson.*

Detail of "Geometric Or Old Hippies Never Die." *Courtesy of Trish Johnson.*

Wooly Friends

With rug makers feeling a close bond to the barnyard friends that produce the wool they hook with, it is only natural and fitting for them to honor sheep.

Accepting the challenge to create an entry to "Sheeptacular Pittsfield," Massachusetts' own Cara Petricca-Carnevale submitted "By Hook or By Crook." Cara's three months of hooking, six to nine hours a day, were attached to a fiberglass form, sprayed with an auto sealant, shellacked with a waterproof glaze, and then displayed for all to see. Designed and hooked by Cara Petricca-Carnevale. Massachusetts. 2004. 60" x 48". *Courtesy of Cara Petricca-Carnevale. Photos courtesy of Kevin Sprague — Studio Two.*

In spite of having six operations for degenerative arthritis and caring for sick parents, Dianne Landberg completed "Night Watch" in time for the annual hooked rug show at the High Desert Museum in Oregon. Hung prominently in the facility's two-story stone entry, the handsome work was the first to greet all visitors. Inspiration to hook a flock of sheep at night came during her trips to and from Oregon to her parents' home in Washington state. There she collected woolen fabrics and shared the excitement of the project with her mother. Designed and hooked by Dianne Landberg. Oregon. 2003. 40" x 40". *Courtesy of Dianne Landberg.*

Sheep belonging to Canadian rug hooking teacher Freda MacDonnell were the motivation behind the hooking of this woolly foursome. "Freda's Friends." Designed by Ariel Baker. Dogwood Hooked Art pattern. Hooked by Anne Hoffman. Kansas. 2004. 17" x 30". *Courtesy of Ariel Baker – Dogwood Hooked Art.*

"Flora," a sheep that needs to be sheared. In addition to the traditional technique of rug hooking, prodding was used to form the sheep's abundant body and decorative flowers. Designed by Victoria Hart Ingalls. Victoria Hart Ingalls pattern. Hooked by JoAn Woody. Missouri. 2003. 15.5" x 19.5". *Courtesy of JoAn Woody.*

The aforementioned "Flora" takes the form of a pillow. Designed by Victoria Hart Ingalls. Victoria Hart Ingalls pattern. Hooked by Cathe Evans. Missouri. 2002. 11" x 14". *Courtesy of Cathe Evans.*

Diamonds, triangles, and simplistic flowers surround a stout "Compton Ram." Designed by Sue Hamer. House of Price / Charco pattern. Hooked by Tricia Travis. Texas. 2004. 28" x 36". *Courtesy of Tricia Travis.*

For added decoration, felt lamb's tongue borders were sometimes sewn along the outside edges of hooked rugs. In this case, hooked lamb's tongues form an inside border framing "The Shade Tree." Fredericksburg Rugs pattern. Hooked by Melissa A. Day. Rhode Island. 2003. 25" x 37". *Courtesy of Melissa A. Day.*

"While in Germany I visited a walled city dating back to the eleventh century. 'Resting Sheep' were in the doorway." Designed and hooked by Theresa Strack. New Hampshire. 2003. 16" x 18". *Courtesy of Theresa Strack.*

Rest your weary head while counting sheep. A soft and cozy hooked "Sheep Pillow" makes that an easy job. Designed by Victoria Hart Ingalls. Victoria Hart Ingalls pattern. Hooked by Lorraine B. Beaver. Missouri. 2005. 18" x 18". *Courtesy of Lorraine B. Beaver.*

And…let us not forget goats. In addition to their being farm animal favorites, it is the under belly wool of cashmere goats that is used to weave the luxurious fabric of the same name. If you can afford to buy yardage, or if given the pricey clothing to recycle into a rug, you will find that hooking with cashmere is a sheer joy.

"I designed this rug for my son. He has pygmy goats and Minnie was his favorite. Minnie thought Jeff was his mother because he helped deliver her. He could walk outside and Minnie would call him: 'Jefffff.' It sounded like she was calling his name." "Minnie's Meadow," complete with white dove, memorializes a special pet. Designed and hooked by Shirley M. Dillard. Georgia. 2005. 33" x 32". *Courtesy of Shirley* M. *Dillard.*

"My best friend and I raised and milked goats while our children were little. Nanny goats are funny, a little crazy, and wonderful companions as farm animals go. Bucks are a different story. They are smelly and strong and give new meaning to the word 'lusty.' My friend decided to get a buck because every year we would pack up all our females and take them to 'visit' the local stud. It got to be a real challenge since each of them came into heat at a different time. My goat liked to ride up in the front seat of the station wagon with me. Anyway she got Goliath. He was quite a specimen. He drooled excitement (and lots of other stuff) from every conceivable orifice if he got within a half mile of a female in heat. His enthusiasm was really noteworthy and we always felt had there been an Olympics in Goliath's sport he would have set world records. As my husband says, 'there is no shame in being called an old goat.' I decided he needed to be memorialized after his long busy life was over, so I surprised my friend with this rug for Christmas." "Goliath – King of the Goats." Designed and hooked by Chris Gooding. Connecticut. 1997. 22" x 27.5". *Courtesy of Chris Gooding.*

Caraway Rug School – Asheboro, North Carolina

Hollywood costumer turned rug hooking artist, Georgia's own Eric Sandberg knows a thing or two about Southern hospitality. Each year during the third week in June, Sandberg acts as director and gracious host for rug hookers who travel to Asheboro to attend his popular five-day long Caraway Rug School. Besides attending an array of classes taught by top notch hooking instructors, listening to guest speakers, and visiting the "camp" store, students can attend and/or participate in the annual flea market, auction, and rug exhibit. Rug hookers enjoy three delicious meals a day, savor afternoon snacks of fresh fruit and chocolate, and are encouraged to relax and enjoy the comfortable accommodations set in the scenic, cool, and wooded North Carolina landscape. Without a doubt, a good time is had by all.

Left:
Pictured is the 2006 brochure for Eric Sandberg's Caraway Rug School, where hooking classes and overnight accommodations are conveniently located under one roof. *Courtesy of Eric Sandberg.*

Hooking teacher Dot Schutte confers with Caraway Rug School director, Eric Sandberg. 2005. *Courtesy of Eric Sandberg.*

The 2005 Roster of Caraway Teachers

A varying roster of teachers, brought in from across the United States, offers expertise in specific areas of rug hooking. There is something for everyone, from beginners to those who have been hooking for thirty or more years.

Dot Schutte color plans a student's rug. 2005. *Courtesy of Eric Sandberg.*

To achieve a special effect, Jeanne Benjamin advises her student to use hand-dyed woolen fabrics. 2005. *Courtesy of Eric Sandberg.*

Jane King addresses questions about technique. 2005. *Courtesy of Eric Sandberg.*

Arms laden with a variety of wools, Diane Stoffel offers background suggestions. 2005. *Courtesy of Eric Sandberg.*

As students look on, an agile Bryan Hancock points out what needs to be hooked next. 2005. *Courtesy of Eric Sandberg.*

Sibyl Osicka discusses one of her latest projects; a hooked tribute to Africa. 2005. *Courtesy of Eric Sandberg.*

A look Inside the 2005 Caraway Classes

Students from near and far enroll in classes to hone their craft and share the joys of hooking.

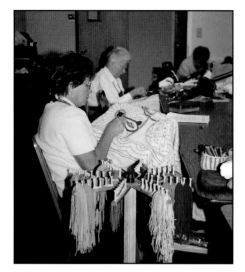

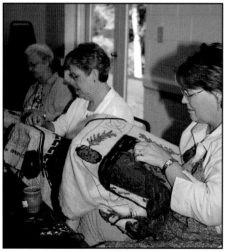

Hooking artists at work. 2005. *Courtesy of Eric Sandberg.*

Each year, rug hooking artists and teachers Nancy and Fred Blair, owners of Michigan's Tomorrow's Heirlooms, pack up a truckload of hooking supplies and head for North Carolina. The popular vendors set up shop at the Caraway Rug School and offer a steady stream of customers everything a rug hooker could ever want. If it's not on the truck, they'll ship it as soon as possible. Nancy holds up a sample of the woolen yardage that she hand-dyes and sells. 2005. *Courtesy of Nancy Blair - Tomorrow's Heirlooms.*

Exhibit

Students and teachers, plus Caraway's director, Eric Sandberg, display their hooked work in an exhibit that is open to the public. The many visitors often become "hooked" themselves and end up enrolling in the following year's school.

The Caraway Center's largest conference room was filled to capacity with hooked work of every size, shape, and subject. 2005. *Courtesy of Eric Sandberg.*

A reposed "Fera" kept a watchful eye on all who visited the 2005 Caraway Rug School exhibit. The portrait pays tribute to a rescued cat. Designed and hooked by Barbara Furmanski. North Carolina. 2004. 13" x 18". *Courtesy of Barbara Furmanski*

Using already cut strips of wool from his "snarl" bag, Caraway Rug School director, hooking artist, and teacher Eric Sandberg fashioned a miniature "Persian Garden." Weft and warp threads from the rug's foundation were used to create the decorative fringe. Designed by Pearl McGown. W. Cushing and Company pattern. Hooked by Eric Sandberg. Georgia. 2004. 14" x 23". *Courtesy of Eric Sandberg.*

Rug hookers often embrace cultural traditions. "The 'Moravian Love Feast' is the tradition of breaking bread together, signifying fellowship, love, and unity. Each person is given a lighted candle with red trimming, a cup of coffee, and a roll." Designed by Jane McGown Flynn. House of Price / Charco pattern. Hooked by Dorothy Lipson. North Carolina. 2005. 16.5" x 19". *Courtesy of Dorothy Lipson.*

A close-up look at Barbara Crawford's "Floral Fantasy" showcases the talents of a seasoned rug hooking artist. Reproduction of a "very old burlap pattern." Pattern maker unknown. Hooked by Barbara Crawford. Maryland. 1997. Actual rug size 30.5" x 50". *Courtesy of Barbara Crawford.*

"After living in our home for 24 years, we have just completed major renovations. This rug kept me sane during this upheaval because it is such a 'happy rug.' Every time I thought I couldn't look at sub-flooring, gutted bathrooms, etc., any longer, I picked up this rug and got lost in the fun of hooking it." "No Evil in Paradise." Designed by "Debbie." Fleecewood Farm pattern. Hooked by Jan King. South Carolina. 2005. 21" x 33". *Courtesy of Jan King.*

Above left, and left:
Decorative pillows, table mats, and wall hangings were among the many hooked items on display. *Courtesy of Eric Sandberg.*

A hooked impressionistic view of "Le Chateau." House of Price / Charco pattern. Hooked by Eric Sandberg. Georgia. 1999. 19" x 25". *Courtesy of Eric Sandberg.*

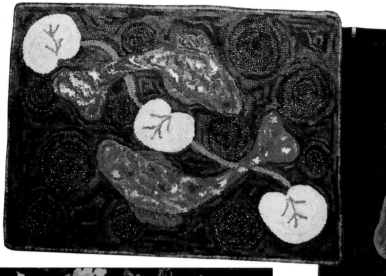

"Fish Pond" koi, raised and sculptured, swim in waters embellished with metallic cording. Designed by Marie Sugar. House of Price / Charco pattern. Hooked by Judy Quintman. North Carolina. 2004. 19" x 26.5". *Courtesy of Judy Quintman.*

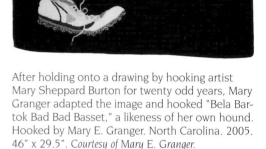

A close-up look at Joy Reich's hooked "Strawberry Patch." Carefully shaded fruit, foliage, and flowers makes for a life-like study. Heirloom Rugs pattern. Hooked by Joy Reich. North Carolina. 1995. Actual rug size 22" x 38". *Courtesy of Joy Reich.*

After holding onto a drawing by hooking artist Mary Sheppard Burton for twenty odd years, Mary Granger adapted the image and hooked "Bela Bartok Bad Bad Basset," a likeness of her own hound. Hooked by Mary E. Granger. North Carolina. 2005. 46" x 29.5". *Courtesy of Mary E. Granger.*

A "Star Struck" kitty, complete with a red feathered friend, brings a note of patriotic cheer. Note the interesting mosaic-like background. Patsy Becker pattern. Hooked by Trudy Jackson. Virginia. 2004. 18" x 25". *Courtesy of Trudy Jackson.*

Sloane King, invited guest, helpmate, and granddaughter of rug hooking artist and teacher Jane King, concentrates on her work. Rug hooking is a King family tradition at which the talented Sloane excels. *Courtesy of Eric Sandberg.*

Hook and Wear Fashions

What better way to display your hooked art than to wear it? Available in a rainbow of colors, clothing hooked of woolen fabric is not only warm and fashionable, it is sure to start up a conversation. "Is that Dorr you're wearing?" (With all due respects to the haute couture House of Dior, most rug hooking enthusiasts prefer to wear Dorr wool from The Dorr Mill Store in Guild, New Hampshire.)

Susie Stephenson makes a fashion statement wearing her own hooked creation. Using her imagination, the images of rugs she has hooked, and the likenesses of her children's drawings, she created "Menagerie Coat," which took over a year to plan. The actual hooking process took six weeks. "I was a woman possessed." The five pound coat (the equivalent of wearing four sweaters) was crafted from recycled woolen clothing. Labels, removed from the clothing, decorate the silk embroidered lining. Designed and hooked by Susie Stephenson. Maine. 2005. Size medium. *Courtesy of Susie Stephenson.*

And what do you wear with a hooked coat of many colors? Monogrammed hooked clogs of course! Designed and hooked by Susie Stephenson. Maine. 2006. *Courtesy of Susie Stephenson.*

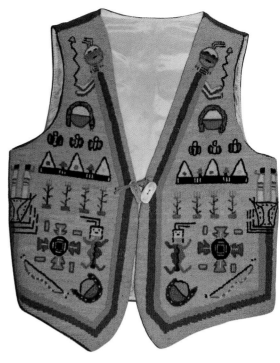

Bound with pigskin, Norma Gillette's hooked "Navajo Vest" reflects traditional Indian symbols. "I hooked one side of the vest deciding on motifs as I went—then the fun began—making the other side to match." A leather tie secures deer antler buttons. Designed and hooked by Norma Gillette. Oregon. 1995. *Courtesy of Norma Gillette.*

Hooked art is not only fashionable, it can be functional as well.

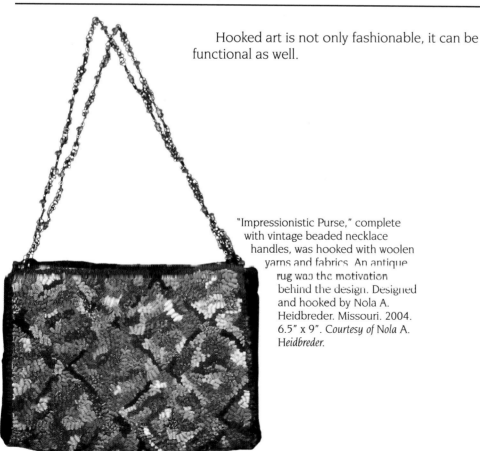

"Impressionistic Purse," complete with vintage beaded necklace handles, was hooked with woolen yarns and fabrics. An antique rug was the motivation behind the design. Designed and hooked by Nola A. Heidbreder. Missouri. 2004. 6.5" x 9". *Courtesy of Nola A. Heidbreder.*

A fashion favorite for fans of our feathered friends. "Bird House Purse." "I like being able to make art that can be utilized." Designed by Susan Mackey. Hooked by Sharon K. Laufer. Vermont. 2000. 6" x 6". *Courtesy of Sharon K. Laufer.*

Computer generated art and a favorite summer handbag inspired Kathleen Betts Boozan's "Hooked Shoulder Bag." Designed and hooked by Kathleen Betts Boozan. Vermont. 2004. 10" x 9". *Courtesy of Kathleen Betts Boozan.*

Taking a trip to the shore? Don't forget to pack your "Fishy Shoulder Bag," suitable for both casual and formal occasions. Designed and hooked by Gail Majauckas. Massachusetts. 2004. 10" x 11". *Courtesy of Gail Majauckas.*

Minimize your hooked art and wear it as jewelry. The original "My Little Sheepie" was "an attempt at creating an old-looking primitive rug, made of wide, hand-torn strips of woolen fabrics and cotton homespun." The miniaturized, wearable version was "made using a Russian punch needle and the finest wool threads I could get." Both designed and hooked by Linda Repasky. Massachusetts. 2004. 14" x 19" and 2" x 2". *Courtesy of Linda Repasky.*

The Dorr Mill Store –
Guild, New Hampshire

In 1967, Pearl McGown, America's grand dame of rug hooking, persuaded mill owner George Dorr to produce a "full, color-matched line of 100% wools for hooking and braiding." Forty years later, under the direction of son Terry, The Dorr Mill Store is still the only source in America for this complete rug wool line. Whether you are visiting the store, ordering by mail, or shopping online, Dorr offers everything any rug hooker could ever want…and more.

Great Things are in Store

Welcome to the meadow. Explore. Enjoy. Gather ideas to make or give. Dorr's open year 'round. A truly unique shopping experience awaits you.

Dorr Lore

We're here by popular request. In 1965 several Dorr Woolen employees who loved to sew asked management for the opportunity to purchase the beautiful wool fabrics made at the mill. Shortly afterwards, in a small corner of the mill, the Dorr Store opened for business. Space was limited so husbands were requested to wait outside. Word about the store spread quickly.

Within a year a new store was built across the street. Then more additions. Over the years a wide selection of fabrics, sportswear, crafts, blankets, and accessories were added.

Our lovely woolens are still available year 'round and you'll always find reasonable wool remnants from the mill. But now there are so many more reasons for coming to Dorr—and reasons to return. For the seasons change and so do we.

For rug hookers, all roads lead to Guild, New Hampshire—home of The Dorr Mill Store. *Courtesy of The Dorr Mill Store.*

—— Cindy Trick – Beavercreek, Ohio ——

With a fondness for folk art, Cindy Trick prefers to hook her rugs in a primitive style, using strips of woolen fabric cut 6/32" or 8/32" wide. Blessed with a special zeal for life and boundless enthusiasm for her craft, she has been happily hooking for twenty years and teaching for ten.

All photos courtesy of Larry Bosley.

Rug makers in the mid-1800s would sometimes use onion skins to dye the fabrics they hooked with. When dyed over a light color, such as white or ivory, the result was mottled shades of gold. "Early Threshold," an antique look-a-like, boasts period decorative motifs and authentic coloration. Heirloom Rugs pattern. Hooked by Cindy Trick. Ohio. 2001. 26" x 38". *Courtesy of Cindy Trick.*

Mimicking nineteenth century rug makers, Cindy Trick hooked cut strips of an antique paisley shawl into the scrolls and flowers of "Old Nutfield." Designed by Ruth R. Hall. W. Cushing and Company pattern. Hooked by Cindy Trick. Ohio. 2002. 31" x 58". *Courtesy of Cindy Trick.*

Decorative stars and vivid patriotic shields add a note of light-hearted whimsy to a somewhat somber traditional motif. "Patriotic Flowerpot." Designed by Cherylyn Brubaker. Hooked Treasures pattern. Hooked by Cindy Trick. Ohio. 2002. 26" x 34.5". *Courtesy of Cindy Trick.*

"Stars, Hearts, and Diamonds Antique" compiles design elements from several century old rugs. Designed and hooked by Cindy Trick. Ohio. 1999. 25" x 36". *Courtesy of Cindy Trick.*

Being of independent spirit, Cindy Trick hooked her "Yellow Basket" pattern with red woolen fabric and bits of paisley shawl. Utilizing the old technique of "clipping," the tops of the hooked loops were cut off, giving the folk art flowers a dense, velvety look and feel. The braiding around the edge echoes the colors hooked within. Designed by Edyth O'Neill. Woolley Fox pattern. Hooked by Cindy Trick. Ohio. 2003. 16" x 19.5". *Courtesy of Cindy Trick.*

Below:

These lively "Six Stars" were adapted from a contemporary folk art painting by Margaret Shaw. Spruce Ridge pattern. Hooked by Cindy Trick. Ohio. 2003. 31" x 58". *Courtesy of Cindy Trick.*

Poised in an abstract sky, the winter moon and stars look down on a cabin-visiting moose. A border, hooked from plaid woolen fabric, frames the "Night Caller." Designed by Emma Lou Lais. Emma Lou Lais pattern. Hooked by Cindy Trick. Ohio. 1997. 24" x 34.5". *Courtesy of Cindy Trick.*

"Folk Art Bunny," adapted from a wood carving and hooked with solid and tweed woolen fabrics, recalls a child's pull toy from days gone by. Designed and hooked by Cindy Trick. Ohio. 1998. 29" x 29". *Courtesy of Cindy Trick.*

Forest Friends

Out of the forest and onto the rugs. Sightings of moose, deer, and fox have been plentiful this hooking season.

"This rug was inspired by a photo my husband Jim took while resting after a long day of hunting. He was down in a bluff with his camera in hand and looking up, took a picture of this beautiful elk as dusk was setting in the background." "Elk at Dusk" is silhouetted against a variegated sky. Adapted from a photo and made into a pattern by Jyl Clark. Hooked by Alice Ann Pearce. Indiana. 2005. 25" x 35". *Courtesy of Alice Ann Pearce.*

Trees, in full fall colors, form a canopy above a resting "Deer in the Woods." Adapted from a Currier and Ives print. Jacqueline Designs pattern. Hooked by Karen Detrick. Ohio. 2002. 14" x 18". *Courtesy of Karen Detrick.*

Hand-dyed woolen fabrics cut into 3/32" wide strips were used to hook and finely shade "Solitude." The woodland scene evokes a sense of peace and tranquility, but according to Alayne Riddle, "it was a challenge." Designed by Jane McGown Flynn. House of Price / Charco pattern. Hooked by Alayne Riddle. Missouri. 1997. 24" x 36". *Courtesy of Alayne Riddle.*

This scene of two deer was adapted from the center motif of an 8' x 10' rug designed and hooked by Gardner King in 1963. Inspired by her late father's work, Rosalie Lent hooked her own version of the frolicking pair. "Gardner King's Deer." Designed by Gardner King. Hooked by Rosalie Lent. Maine. 2005. 15" x 18". *Courtesy of Rosalie Lent.*

Anatomical changes and a bed of flowers were added to enhance a favorite Edward Sands Frost (1843-1894) pattern. "Reindeer with Oak Leaves." "GV85." W. Cushing and Company pattern. Hooked by Lettie Conrad. Vermont. 1996. 30" x 56". *Courtesy of Lettie Conrad.*

"Old Chalk Deer" was modeled after an antique figurine. A primitive rope border and leafy scrolls add period decoration. Designed by Edyth O'Neill. Woolley Fox pattern. Hooked by Rose Mary Kircher. Texas. 2001. 29" x 36". *Courtesy of Rose Mary Kircher.*

Curlicue scrolls and angular borders frame a stately stag's head. Edward Sands Frost pattern. "GV80." W. Cushing and Company pattern. Hooked by Bette Bryant. Texas. 2004. 23" x 34.5". *Courtesy of Bette Bryant.*

"In the Woods" was designed for "primitive (style) hookers who hook simplified forms and shapes that are not too small, and who have a preference for North country wildlife." Designed by Chris Lewis. Dogwood Hooked Art pattern. Hooked by Anne Hoffman. Missouri. 2004. 23" x 27.5". *Courtesy of Dogwood Hooked Art and Anne Hoffman.*

A balancing act, the likes of which you would never see in nature. "Animals in the Woods" was given as a gift to "a good friend who is director of our county's Outdoor Education Program." Beverly Conway Designs pattern. Hooked by Susan Naples. California. 2004. 30" x 21". *Courtesy of Susan Naples.*

"Bear Country." Capturing fish and memories of trips to Alaska. Adapted from an illustration on a popcorn tin. Jacqueline Designs pattern. Hooked by Karen Detrick. Ohio. 2004. 20" x 18". *Courtesy of Karen Detrick.*

We all know someone who is a bear until that "First Sip" of coffee. A comical hooked comment about human traits and forest animals. Designed by Ariel Baker. Dogwood Hooked Art pattern. Hooked by Chris Lewis. Missouri. 2005. 21" x 21". *Courtesy of Chris Lewis – Dogwood Hooked Art.*

Detail of "Animals in the Woods." *Courtesy of Susan Naples.*

Twisting and turning vines, laden with Halloween ready pumpkins, contain a watchful fox. Note the orange "escapees" rolling into the outer border. "Fox and Pumpkins." Dogwood Hooked Art pattern. Hooked by Minerva D. Cabanas. Kansas. 2004. 24" x 36". *Courtesy of Minerva D. Cabanas*

"When designing 'Fox and Pumpkins' I wanted to surround the fox with circle shapes and warm fall colors. With all the 'busyness' of the pumpkins and vines, the broad border is meant to be simple." Dogwood Hooked Art pattern. Designed and hooked by Chris Lewis. Missouri. 1995. 24" x 36". *Courtesy of Chris Lewis – Dogwood Hooked Art.*

Victoria Hart Ingalls – Independence, Missouri

Known for her focus on fine shading, attention to detail, and portraiture, Victoria Hart Ingalls is a much-in-demand rug hooking instructor in her Independence home and at rug hooking schools across the country. Having hooked for thirty years and taught for nearly twenty, she has a fine arts degree and studied under the late Margaret Hunt Masters, a well-known rug hooking teacher and author. Her award winning work, as well as her written expertise, has appeared in several rug hooking publications. Victoria Hart Ingalls…a lovely lady whose delicate and refined hooked art is a delight to behold.

In addition to the following, other examples of Victoria Hart Ingalls' work and patterns can be found throughout this book.

"This was first designed as a wood carving pattern for my husband, Tom, to do on a footstool for a student of mine at the 'Show-Me Rug School' in Atchison, Kansas. She made a request for a rose and a hook. I liked it so much we have used it on the cover of my pattern catalog and business cards." "Victoria's Rose." Designed by Victoria Hart Ingalls. Victoria Hart Ingalls pattern. Hooked by Victoria Hart Ingalls. Missouri. 1996. 8.5" x 12.5". *Courtesy of Victoria Hart Ingalls.*

"My husband Tom and I spent a day in Natchez, Mississippi, on the way home from my teaching at the Plantation Workshop in St. Francisville, Louisiana. Browsing through an antique store I found a child's rocker dated 1850. Upon bringing it home, it seemed to deserve a special chair pad. After all, it had survived the Civil War. I found Margaret Hunt Master's 'Violet Corsage' in my colletion and it was the right size. What a joy to hook one of her designs again after all this time. She was my teacher, mentor, and friend." Designed by Margaret Hunt Masters. Hooked by Victoria Hart Ingalls. Missouri. 2005. Diameter 9.5". *Courtesy of Victoria Hart Ingalls.*

"I admired this piece in Margaret Master's family room for years—finally I decided to hook the pattern myself." "Blythe Shoals." Designed by Margaret Hunt Masters. Prairie Craft House pattern. Hooked by Victoria Ingalls. Missouri. 1995. 30" x 35". *Courtesy of Victoria Hart Ingalls.*

"Kitten with Violets" was "complicated but fun, because the tiny tweed used looked just like the fur on the only cat I ever raised from a kitten, Evie Joy." Designed by Victoria Hart Ingalls. Victoria Hart Ingalls pattern. Hooked by Victoria Hart Ingalls. Missouri. 1996. 6" x 5.5". *Courtesy of Victoria Hart Ingalls.*

"My grandmother collected little watercolors portraits from the turn of the last century. The ones that are dated range from about 1900-1910. I think it was fashionable at the time for young ladies to learn to paint. This hooked portrait was inspired by one of them, but in the watercolor version the girl was holding a bull dog. It was a much better painting of the dog than the girl so I made no attempt at creating a likeness of her. I also decided to put a kitten in my picture. This is another pattern I've never offered for sale. It would be too hard to duplicate as I did so much 'painting' from the scrap bag." "Young Girl with Kitten." Designed and hooked by Victoria Hart Ingalls. Missouri. 1999. 21.5" x 17.5". *Courtesy of Victoria Hart Ingalls.*

"I bought a note card in Williamsburg, Virginia, by nineteenth century artist Henrietta Ronner Knipp of a mother cat and kittens. I just fell in love with the picture and later decided to hook the mother cat and finish it off as a little dummy board. She usually sits on top of my fireplace mantle." Designed and hooked by Victoria Hart Ingalls. Missouri. 1995. 6" x 9". *Courtesy of Victoria Hart Ingalls.*

"Baby Chick and a Crocus" was a "mini class project so my students could learn to do the plaid border." Designed by Victoria Hart Ingalls. Victoria Hart Ingalls pattern. Hooked by Victoria Hart Ingalls. Missouri. 1999. 6" x 8". *Courtesy of Victoria Hart Ingalls.*

"A number of years ago, my mother found a file in the basement that her mother had kept from the 1930s on rug hooking. It contained many interesting clippings and the pattern of this cat. It was my first attempt at a wider cut and I was only willing to go up to a #5." The finer the woolen fabric is cut, the more detail a rug hooker can achieve. Based on 1/32 of an inch, a #5 cut is 5/32", a #4 is 4/32" wide, and so on. Victoria generally prefers to hook with #3. Once hooked, the vintage cat pattern was used to cover a footstool. Name of pattern and pattern maker unknown. Hooked by Victoria Hart Ingalls. Missouri. 1998. 12" x15". *Courtesy of Victoria Hart Ingalls.*

Inspired by a design on an antique sterling silver thimble, "I taught a 'Thimble Birds' mini-class because my students loved it so." Designed by Linda Brown. Hooked by Victoria Hart Ingalls. Missouri. 2000. 8.5" x 23". *Courtesy of Victoria Hart Ingalls.*

"'The Little Patriot' is very special to me. He represents the sacrifice our forefathers made that we might enjoy the freedom we do today. You might notice the name of my hometown and Harry Truman's—Independence. What a patriotic address. On the square, for many, many years was a little bakery and sandwich shop with very old floor tile (linoleum) in patriotic designs. It was so old some of the pattern was completely gone. This little soldier was still left. He inspired my rug design but I felt he needed a flag and stars. My husband told me to make one of the flowers on the ground a forget-me-not so we don't EVER forget the revolution. It was completed on July 4th, 2000." Designed by Victoria Hart Ingalls. Victoria Hart Ingalls pattern. Hooked by Victoria Hart Ingalls. Missouri. 2000. 20" x 24". *Courtesy of Victoria Hart Ingalls.*

"Tom (my husband) printed a tiny, very blurry picture of just the chicken for me one day from an antique postcard he found on the Internet. The Easter egg tree was his idea and I felt she needed a purple crocus and a snowdrop to show it was spring. I drew her freehand and don't know how close she is to the original since it was so indistinct. The postcard was only inspiration. 'Henrietta' is one of my favorite pieces. She's done in a #6 cut (6/32") with lots of shading. I looked at her across the room one day and thought to myself, 'Henrietta' is fine hooking with wide cut.' She was such fun to hook." Designed by Victoria Hart Ingalls. Victoria Hart Ingalls pattern. Hooked by Victoria Hart Ingalls. Missouri. 2003. 17" x 21". *Courtesy of Victoria Hart Ingalls.*

Victoria Hart Ingalls and her mother stand beside Ruth's "French Rug." Inspired by an Aubusson carpet in France's Palace of Versailles, the off and on again project took twenty years to complete. Following family tradition, Ruth, who has been hooking for over thirty years, was first introduced to rug making by her mother. Designed by Margaret Hunt Masters. Hooked by Ruth Trainor Hart. Missouri. 1999. 10' 5" x 8' 5". *Courtesy of Ruth Trainor Hart.*

The Hook and I –
Mount Desert Island, Maine

When Patricia Wharton's hooked rugs were exhibited during the winter of 2003, several other residents of Maine's Mount Desert Island took notice and wanted hooking lessons. The self-taught Ms. Wharton convinced those interested that "they could come together in a collegial atmosphere to learn from one another." "The Hook and I" was formed, and the group's dozen or so members continue an annual island tradition of putting their work on display. In the words of Ms. Wharton, "Some started out with purchased patterns or kits, while others have created original designs from the start. Some use wool yarns; others cut wool strips. Some rugs exhibit a traditional bold composition; others are more complicated and subtly executed. A few members grew up on the island, watching mothers and grandmothers ply the hook. Others of the group are 'first generation' craftswomen. There is always a variety of color, subject, and technique, which makes this an exciting group to be part of."

A sampling of the group's hooked art follows.

"When we moved to Maine, I changed my career from social worker to antique dealer. I found this piece of burlap in an antique store along the coast. It was a rug 'all marked out,' as early rug patterns were called. As I buy and sell a lot of hooked rugs in my business, I decided it would be fun to do a patterned one. I was surprised to find so much freedom in using a pattern—the freedom of color choice." "Floral Hooked Rug." Name of pattern and pattern maker unknown. Hooked by Judith Burger Gossart. Maine. 2004. 27" x 40". *Courtesy of Judith Burger Gossart.*

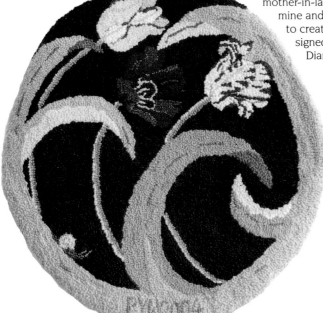

"'Art Nouveau Tulips' is patterned after a silver and onyx pendant my mother-in-law designed and executed in 1939. The pendant is now mine and I wear it often. Her tulips are closed. I opened these up to create depth and to add color." Hooked with wool yarns. Designed and hooked by Patricia Yearout Wharton. Maine. 2004. Diameter 23.5". *Courtesy of Patricia Yearout Wharton.*

"Narcissi." "I created this floral motif as a companion rug to 'Art Nouveau Tulips,' using the same colors for the leaves and background, the same number of blossoms, and another spring flower that grows from a bulb." Hooked with wool yarns. Designed and hooked by Patricia Yearout Wharton. Maine. 2004. Diameter 23.5". *Courtesy of Patricia Yearout Wharton.*

"As a young lady, I used to watch my mother hook rugs and it always fascinated me. After moving on in life, marriage, and having children, I forgot about learning and hooking until retirement. I then started thinking about what I would like to do for myself and immediately knew that I would really like to learn to hook rugs with yarn. It just came so naturally." "Summer Outing" took four months to complete and was made for an avid canoeist husband. Hooked with wool yarns. Designed and hooked by Suzanne Mitchell. Maine. 2004. 54" x 30". *Courtesy of Suzanne Mitchell.*

"My husband's grandparents were rug hookers. I looked at some of their rugs we had inherited and was impressed! This is something I can do, I thought, so I took a rug hooking class and found that I really enjoyed hooking rugs. I find this a relaxing and enjoyable way to spend my spare time, especially during the long winter months here in Maine." "Schooner." Designed by Christine Sherman for Searsport Rug Hooking. Hooked by Pamela D. Bicknell. Maine. 2004. 24" x 36". *Courtesy of Pamela D. Bicknell.*

"This rug was hooked in the winter of 2004. It was my 'therapy' during a most difficult time in my life that necessitated many trips to specialists in Boston and protracted stays away from home. Happily, like 'The Schooner Judith' my husband and I finally sailed into calmer waters and a safe harbor." Designed and hooked by Judith Burger Gossart. Maine. 2004. 34" x 48". *Courtesy of Judith Burger Gossart.*

"In my late 20s and 30s I designed and hooked four rugs in keeping with a family tradition—my mother and then my father, after his retirement, designed and made original hooked rugs. For thirty years I did other things, but gradually began to feel the pull to hook again. This desire coincided with the formation of a rug hooking group here on Mount Desert Island. What design to make? We had a beloved Airedale, 'Fred,' who was a born companion: always steadfast, joyous, and ready for any gambit. He was meant to be a show dog but we never went that route. Fred was our 5 star dog and at the time I hooked the rug he was facing his sunset years." Designed and hooked by Judith Burger Gossart. Maine. 2003. 25" x 34". *Courtesy of Judith Burger Gossart.*

"We moved to Mount Desert Island twelve years ago. Our home looks out on the Frenchman Bay and seals are regularly seen swimming by, perching on our ledge, or—occasionally in winter—floating by on a small piece of ice. A move is a risky business, but our move to Mount Desert Island was just right for us and won my 'Seal of Approval.' "Frenchman Bay Seal of Approval." Designed and hooked by Judith Burger Gossart. Maine. 2004. 29" x 38.5". *Courtesy of Judith Burger Gossart.*

"I began hooking 'Forest Creatures,' a scene reflective of my Maine home's backyard flora and fauna, in January 2003 and completed it March 2005. It was an enjoyable and social pastime, worked actually only during the winter months that our local group, 'The Hook and I' convened." Hooked with wool yarn. Claire Murray pattern and kit. Hooked by Anne Molavi. Maine. 2005. 24" x 36". *Courtesy of Anne Molavi.*

"In the fall of 2002, I attended Maine's Common Ground Fair in Unity, where I saw the teams of oxen put through their paces. Once back home, I couldn't forget the handsome Holstein pair, Beau and Bill. I traced down their owner and obtained photographs. I found two more pair to observe to help me design this rug." "Blue Ribbon Ox," complete with "undulating" awards, is set in a classic English countryside. Hooked with wool yarns. Designed and hooked by Patricia Yearout Wharton. Maine. 2003. 24.5" x 35.5" *Courtesy of Patricia Yearout Wharton.*

"'Blue Border Collie' is 'a companion rug to 'Blue Ribbon Ox,' using a black and white animal and blue ribbon in the border. The setting is inspired by James Herriot (English veterinarian and author of *All Creatures Great and Small*), but I put my collie in Scotland with a castle and sheep. His coat is embellished with silk and nylon knitting yarns." Hooked with wool yarns. Designed and hooked by Patricia Yearout Wharton. Maine. 2004. 24.5" x 35.5". *Courtesy of Patricia Yearout Wharton.*

Carolyn Kilner –
Hooked Points of View

When women were crafting rugs in the latter half of the 1800s, their thoughts and opinions were generally regarded as frivolous and most surely not allowed to be expressed in their hooked handiwork.

Well…times have changed and you've come a long way, baby. Modern women want their opinions known and Canadian hooking artist Carolyn Kilner is no exception.

"If fear can come in a sudden wave, it happened when President Bush declared war on Iraq. Although 9-11 had been a terrible tragedy, and certainly New York is not that far from Toronto—Canadians felt the affects of this terrorist act as well, since many of our downtown buildings were evacuated—we watched the news in horror as many of our families and friends live in the States, some even in New York. It was an unconscionable act of hatred and evil.

"However, something strange occurred. It was assumed that the perpetrator of this heinous outrage would be dealt with and brought to some sort of justice. But President Bush didn't go after Osama Bin Laden, who had orchestrated this atrocity, he declared his war on Saddam Hussein. In that moment, I wasn't sure who the madman really was. To declare war on a nation that hadn't declared war on the United States was insane.

"As a parent, I looked at my four children between the ages of 18 and 22 and realized that if this escalated in any way and included Canada, my children were the right ages to be proclaimed warriors. I felt inconsolable. My children couldn't understand why I was so upset since war is an unreality to them. I reminded them that their cousins were in the States—one joined the army and would probably end up in Iraq—and that you never can calculate how wars will escalate. You don't know if it will involve other countries or not. As a Canadian,

I feel a real affinity to my US neighbors and this is a tragedy for the young who must fight and for their families. Also, I work in a Toronto school and we have many Iraqi students whose families and friends would be living the first hand horror of war. How could I ignore their loss in this? Their relationship would be a target of a country that had no business retaliating against a mythical enemy. Iraq had not bombed the twin towers. Many Americans and Canadians felt the same way. Where was the war against Bin Laden and his henchmen? Our world is a 'global community,' including the innocent on both sides who have and will be wounded. Already this had escalated to unbelievable proportions and continues to do so.

"The question was, how would I work these deep feelings of fear, confusion, and anger out. A rug! So I drew a design with President Bush (the cat) throwing his fishing line over the Bird of Paradise flower and fishing for Saddam Hussein in the fish bowl. In the process of fishing, Bush is pulling over 'Paradise.'

"The third person in the picture is supposed to be Jean Chrétien our (Canadian) former Prime Minister. However, since I am a novice in drawing, my kids thought it was either Richard Nixon or Bob Hope. I made some adjustments but I'm still not sure he's easily recognizable so it is up to the imagination as to who might be in the flower. And yes, Bush has rather large red lips but botox will do that!

"I entitled the piece 'Fissures of Men,' which is a play on the biblical statement that Jesus made to his disciples when he told them that they would be 'Fishers of men.' Leaders need to remember that they are responsible for their decisions and that both Bin Laden and Bush have a lot to account for."

"Fissures of Men – The USA/ Iraqi War." Designed and hooked by Carolyn Kilner. Ontario. Canada. 2004. 52" x 56". *Courtesy of Carolyn Kilner.*

"When my youngest brother divorced, he re-entered our family after a long time of remaining distant to us. I was so overjoyed to come to know him as an adult and as a friend that I made this rug for him. My hope is that he and I will enjoy a long life together as friends and that our children will benefit from that re-union.

"I have long been a fan of women in Indonesia who practice the art of batik. It is a process of layering wax and dyeing fabric until all patterns are on the fabric, creating a design. It requires great skill and artistry. The basic layout of fabric is a border around the whole rectangular piece and then three panels. The first one to the right is a medium sized panel with a design in it. The second panel is smaller and divides the two other panels. The third panel is a large area that mimics the design of the medium sized panel. The cloth is then worn as a wrap-around skirt."

"Long Life." Designed and hooked by Carolyn Kilner. Ontario, Canada. 2001. 32" x 57". *Private collection of Gary Edwards.*

"As women, we play a number of roles. The life-sized pattern pieces represent our multi-faceted identity. The rugs are done on pattern templates to represent our versatility and the needs we meet in our families and communities.

"The *pant piece* has silhouettes of nude bodies on it and since it is a pant pattern piece, the arm of a woman is hung at the side of the pattern. The woman is wearing high heels just as street-walkers would wear. Throughout history, many impoverished and disenfranchised women have resorted to prostitution to survive. However, the purse the prostitute is carrying has a rug hooking handle with a rug hook on it, which represents the traditional resourcefulness of women.

"Although we may not agree with prostitution on a moral basis, we can't forget that many women have little choice in this trade and that their resourcefulness is still commendable. I believe that women throughout the world need to be recognized for their importance, but also for the difficult places they have to walk as well.

"The *top back piece* has the Toronto CN tower on it, but the needle at the top bends into a sewing needle with thread. If you look closely, there is another pattern piece superimposed on the pattern piece. This represents women's ability to look after their families and use their resources to supplement family income.

"The *front dress piece* has been dressed up with jewelry and a wide belt. The dress represents the beauty of women and their ability to adapt and accessorize. Women are not only valued by themselves or others for their abilities and resourcefulness, but for beauty as well. Inner beauty doesn't hide inside. It reflects throughout the whole woman. At the bottom, there is a young women leaning back on a couch enjoying some leisure time. Leisure is not necessarily a commodity that many women have had, but for those who do, a moment with one's self is a valuable and worthwhile moment."

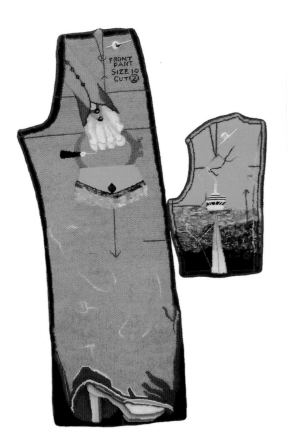
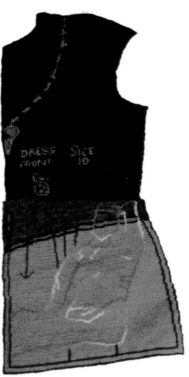

A closer look at "Womyn's Rugs." *Courtesy of Carolyn Kilner.*

"Womyn's Rugs." Designed and hooked by Carolyn Kilner. Ontario, Canada. 2004. Size 10. *Courtesy of Carolyn Kilner.*

The Potted Pear – West Chester, Ohio

When two enterprising rug hooking enthusiasts from Ohio put their heads together, the results can be magical. In 2000, Jenny Rupp and Lisa Yeago, both hooking artists and pattern designers, formed The Potted Pear. Their popular and growing mail order business offers a wide array of folk art patterns for rugs, banners, and dolls; instruction books and DVDs; hand-dyed woolen fabrics and yarns; and so much more. The dynamic duo of Rupp and Yeago can often be found teaching classes, directing workshops, and vending at shows.

The following Potted Pear patterns were designed by Jenny Rupp and Lisa Yeago.

All photos courtesy of Larry Bosley

The Potted Pair catalog offers patterns, helpful hints, and humor. *Courtesy of Jenny Rupp and Lisa Yeago.*

Bringing an antique motif into the twenty-first century. Contained "Circles and Stars" convey a feeling of energy and movement. Potted Pear pattern. Hooked by Jenny Rupp. Ohio. 2005. 24" x 36". *Courtesy of Jenny Rupp.*

"Star and Stripes" combines a traditional basket weave hit or miss stripe with cheerful blocks of stars. A great way to use up leftover wools from other projects. Potted Pear pattern. Hooked by Lisa Yeago. Ohio. 2003. 16" x 24". *Courtesy Lisa Yeago.*

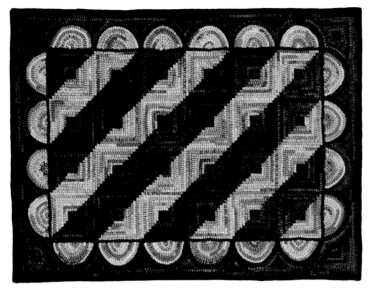

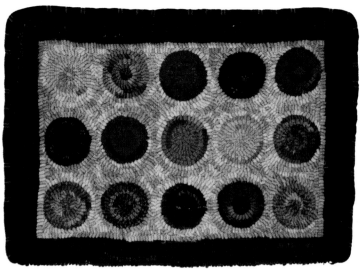

Quilt patterns are easily adapted to hooking patterns and are a favorite among contemporary rug makers. "Log Cabin with Clam Shell Border." Potted Pear pattern. Hooked by Lisa Yeago. Ohio. 2002. 22" x 30". *Courtesy of Lisa Yeago.*

A great beginner's project. Fifteen colorful circles add a note of cheer. "Circles Mat." Potted Pear pattern. Hooked by Jenny Rupp. Ohio. 2001. 12" x 17". *Courtesy of Jenny Rupp.*

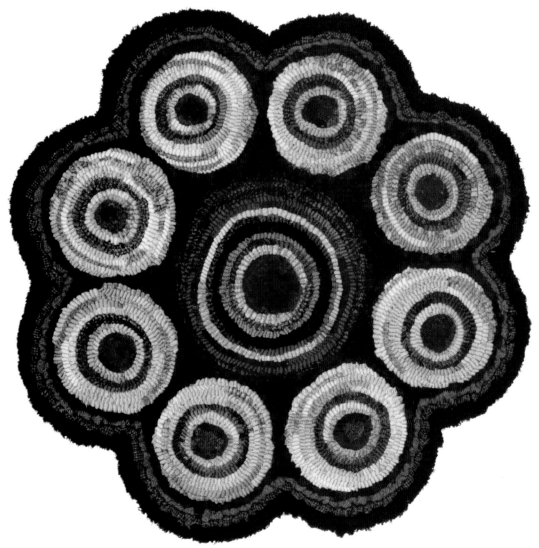

A class given by Missouri's hooking artist, Nola Heidbreder, was the motivation behind the design of "Nola's Rug." In addition to hooking with woolen fabric strips, Jenny Rupp used velvet and chenille yarns when she fashioned her "moving" tribute to circles. Potted Pear pattern. Hooked by Jenny Rupp. Ohio. 2004. Diameter 20". *Courtesy of Jenny Rupp.*

"Lisa's Geometric." An undulating decorative frame rests upon a hit or miss basket weave background, bringing interest and movement to a traditional and often used rug hooking pattern. Potted Pear pattern. Hooked by Lisa Yeago. Ohio. 2003. 20" x 28". *Courtesy of Lisa Yeago.*

Small red squares enhance the optical illusion of a hooked "Log Cabin" quilt pattern. Forming the center of the background squares, these bright notes of color also anchor the shadowed diamonds in the forefront. Potted Pear pattern. Hooked by Jenny Rupp. Ohio. 2001. 24" x 36". *Courtesy of Jenny Rupp.*

After the hooking was completed, an appliquéd wool "flame" was sewn along the edge of this colorful geometric design. Reminiscent of Victorian needlework, the decorative saw tooth border introduces triangles to "Many Squares." Potted Pear pattern. Hooked by Jenny Rupp. Ohio. 2005. 24" X 36". *Courtesy of Jenny Rupp.*

Contained within a linear block border, diagonally hooked lines of color play tricks on the eye and form an ever changing "Geometric" pattern. Potted Pear pattern. Hooked by Jenny Rupp. Ohio. 2000. 30" x 60". *Courtesy of Jenny Rupp.*

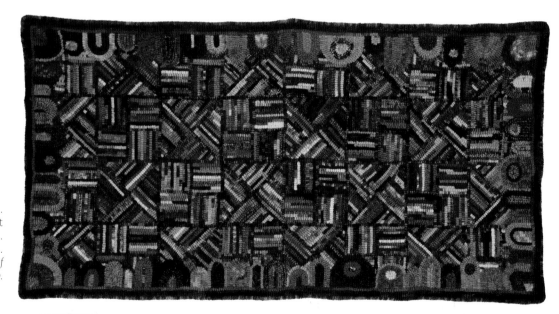

Controlled order and design. "Gone Crazy" is a fun project to hook. Potted Pear pattern. Hooked by Lisa Yeago. Ohio. 2004. 24" x 48". *Courtesy of Lisa Yeago.*

"Sample This" was designed to showcase a variety of woolen fabrics, including those that were dip- and spot-dyed. Hooking with wide cuts (6/32" – 8/32") gives this rug a "primitive" look. Potted Pear pattern. Hooked by Lisa Yeago. Ohio. 2005. 12" x 28". *Courtesy of Lisa Yeago.*

Recalling appliquéd quilts, whimsical borders separate "Baskets and Urns." A continuous floral vine frames the quadrants. Potted Pear pattern. Hooked by Lisa Yeago. Ohio. 2004. 44" x 44". *Courtesy of Lisa Yeago.*

"Strawberry Basket Sampler," a tribute to vintage needlework, also serves as a learning tool for young readers. Note the tablet-shaped design. Potted Pear pattern. Hooked by Lisa Yeago. Ohio. 2005. 28" x 18". *Courtesy of Lisa Yeago.*

A slightly jumbled alphabet is hooked into the background of "Primitive Flower Sampler." Lollipop-like flowers, often seen on antique hooked rugs, are once again popular with modern day rug hookers. Potted Pear pattern. Hooked by Lisa Yeago. Ohio. 2003. 24" x 31". *Courtesy of Lisa Yeago.*

Many rug hookers are attracted to a patriotic palette and themes. "Liberty" is suitable as a floor covering, wall hanging, or table decoration. Potted Pair pattern. Hooked by Lisa Yeago. Ohio. 2004. 16" x 25". *Courtesy of Lisa Yeago.*

A more contemporary hooked "ABC Runner." Potted Pear pattern. Hooked by Lisa Yeago. Ohio. 2003. 11" x 44". *Courtesy of Lisa Yeago.*

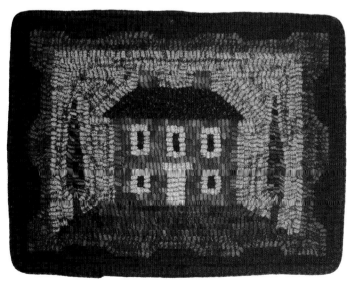

Part of the delightful and charming "Colonial Minis" collection. Top: "Colonial Basket" and "Colonial Eagle." Bottom: "Colonial House" and "Colonial Flower." Potted Pear patterns. Hooked by Lisa Yeago. Ohio. 2005. Each 11" x 14". *Courtesy of Lisa Yeago.*

The Potted Pear's philosophy for a happy life: "Eat More Pie" and "Drink More Coffee." While not sanctioned by leading nutritionists, these whimsical hooked comments have been known to cause spontaneous smiles. Potted Pear patterns. Hooked by Jenny Rupp. Ohio. 2001. Each 18" x 20". *Courtesy of Jenny Rupp.*

Along with size and shape, "Postage Stamp House" borrows the scalloped edge from a stamp and turns it inward to form a frame. Folk art flowers complement the skinny structure and the surname of the artist who hooked it. Potted Pear pattern. Hooked by Jenny Rupp. Ohio. 2005. 18" x 13". *Courtesy of Jenny Rupp.*

Set inside a vintage frame, the "Our Day" pattern allows rug hookers the opportunity to hook in their own special date. A perfect wedding or anniversary gift. Note the stained glass window over the church door. Potted Pear pattern. Hooked by Jenny Rupp. Ohio. 2003. 21" x 15". *Courtesy of Jenny Rupp.*

This smile provoking polka dot barnyard "Hen" is part of a "story" set of patterns called "Which Came First;" "Hen," "Chick," and "Egg." Potted pear pattern. Hooked by Jenny Rupp. Ohio. 2001. 20" x 18". *Courtesy of Jenny Rupp.*

Can't find enough things to hook? How about "Harry Hare – Jar Topper." Once completed, the hooked pattern was sewn together, stuffed, then glued onto the cover of an antique jar. Potted Pear pattern. Hooked by Jenny Rupp. Ohio. 2003. Jar and hare 15" tall. *Courtesy of Jenny Rupp.*

Fashioned after a garden favorite, "Black-Eyed Susan" has a hooked face and a lanky cloth body. Potted Pear pattern. Hooked by Jenny Rupp. Ohio. 2004. 18" tall. *Courtesy of Jenny Rupp.*

Flashing a toothy grin and toting his carrot, this adorable hooked "Hare" is waiting to be cuddled. A simplistic body form, with eyes nearly in his ears, delights both young and old. Potted Pear pattern. Hooked by Jenny Rupp. Ohio. 1999. 18" tall. *Courtesy of Jenny Rupp.*

Offering a wide variety of holiday inspired-patterns, no one embraces the Halloween spirit more than The Potted Pear.

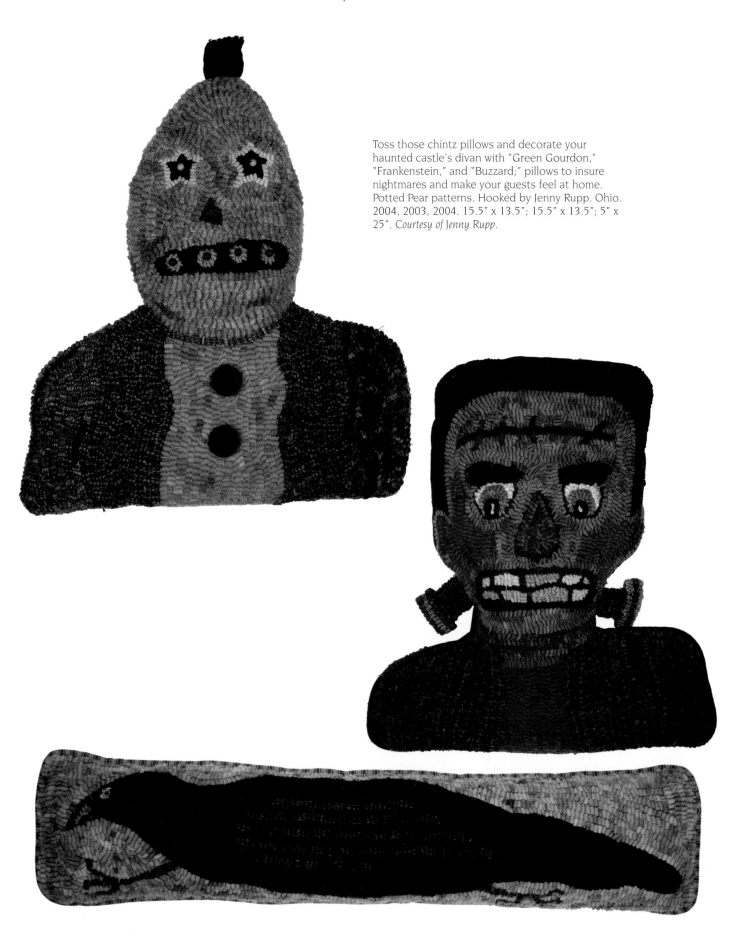

Toss those chintz pillows and decorate your haunted castle's divan with "Green Gourdon," "Frankenstein," and "Buzzard;" pillows to insure nightmares and make your guests feel at home. Potted Pear patterns. Hooked by Jenny Rupp. Ohio. 2004, 2003, 2004. 15.5" x 13.5"; 15.5" x 13.5"; 5" x 25". *Courtesy of Jenny Rupp.*

"Big Jack Pumpkin Shape" complements both cobwebs and cracks—a wall hanging for any dreary drawing room. Potted Pear pattern. Hooked by Jenny Rupp. Ohio. 2003. 18" x 24". *Courtesy of Jenny Rupp.*

Share those family recipes with others and pass out a hooked "Secret Potion." Potted Pear pattern. Hooked by Jenny Rupp. Ohio. 2003. 24" x 15". *Courtesy of Jenny Rupp.*

"Two Hoots." Chevron bands, with Halloween appropriate motifs, flank two branch-sharing owls, each not giving a hoot and looking in a different direction. A striated full moon highlights the pair. Potted Pear pattern. Hooked by Jenny Rupp. Ohio. 2000. 24" x 36". *Courtesy of Jenny Rupp.*

Does your decrepit mansion scream out for an All Hallow's Eve makeover? Interior decorator Morticia Addams highly recommends adding a touch of the morose to that dusty staircase of yours. Rip up an old shroud or two and hook thirteen of The Potted Pear's Halloween stair riser patterns. What better way to enjoy a dreary starless night than hooking in the dark, listening to wolves bay at the moon, and anticipating the reaction of the deceased and the living when they gaze upon your latest hooked handiwork!

All of the following Halloween stair risers are Potted Pear patterns and were hooked in 2003. Each measures 5" x 25".

"Rat Fink." Hooked by Jenny Rupp. *Courtesy of Jenny Rupp.*

"Devil and Cats." Hooked by Jenny Rupp. *Courtesy of Jenny Rupp.*

"October." Hooked by Lisa Yeago. *Courtesy of Lisa Yeago.*

"At the Window." Hooked by Lisa Yeago. *Courtesy of Lisa Yeago.*

"Halloween." Hooked by Lisa Yeago. *Courtesy of Lisa Yeago.*

"Tarantula." Hooked by Jenny Rupp. *Courtesy of Jenny Rupp.*

"Happy Jack." Hooked by Lisa Yeago. *Courtesy of Lisa Yeago.*

"Good To Eat." Hooked by Jenny Rupp. *Courtesy of Jenny Rupp.*

"Floating Ghost." Hooked by Lisa Yeago. *Courtesy of Lisa Yeago.*

"Scaredy-cat." Hooked by Jenny Rupp. *Courtesy of Jenny Rupp.*

"Mummy." Hooked by Lisa Yeago. *Courtesy of Lisa Yeago.*

"Trick or Treat." Hooked by Jenny Rupp. *Courtesy of Jenny Rupp.*

"Witch's Broom." Hooked by Jenny Rupp. *Courtesy of Jenny Rupp.*

"Cauldron." Hooked by Jenny Rupp. *Courtesy of Jenny Rupp.*

"R.I.P." Hooked by Lisa Yeago. *Courtesy of Lisa Yeago.*

"Spider Web." Hooked by Jenny Rupp. *Courtesy of Jenny Rupp.*

"Candy Corn." Hooked by Lisa Yeago. *Courtesy of Lisa Yeago.*

"Sad Jack." Hooked by Jenny Rupp. *Courtesy of Jenny Rupp.*

"3 Jacks." Hooked by Jenny Rupp. *Courtesy of Jenny Rupp.*

"Beware." Hooked by Jenny Rupp. *Courtesy of Jenny Rupp.*

"Big Bat." Hooked by Jenny Rupp. *Courtesy of Jenny Rupp.*

The Newtown Hooked Rug Show – Sandy Hook, Connecticut

In 2001, the Board of Trustees of Connecticut's historical Newtown Meeting House was looking to raise money for its Music Fund. A local antique dealer suggested a hooked rug show, to which Meeting House manager Sherry Paisley said, "What's a hooked rug?" Upon the same dealer's suggestion, Sherry contacted nearby hooking artist, Liz Alpert Fay. Very much interested in putting on an exhibit, the two, with the cooperation of the Goodwives and Nutmeg chapter of ATHA (Association of Traditional Hooking Artists), co-chaired what has become an annual event. With over one hundred hooked works displayed, nearly forty vendors, hooking demonstrations, a raffle, and guest speaker, an eager audience anxiously awaits the much anticipated November show.

THIRD ANNUAL NEWTOWN HOOKED RUG SHOW

Date: Saturday, November 6, 2004

Time: 10:00 A.M. to 4:00 P.M.

Place: Reed Intermediate School
3 Trades Lane
Sandy Hook, Connecticut

Speaker: Jessie A. Turbayne is an internationally recognized authority on hooked rugs, and the author of four highly regarded books which are valued by both collectors

A 2004 flyer announces the Newtown Hooked Rug Show. The yearly November event is supported by the Nutmeg chapter of ATHA (Association of Traditional Hooking Artists) as well as by the Connecticut Commission on Culture and Tourism and the Northwest Connecticut Convention and Visitors Bureau. *Courtesy of the Newtown Hooked Rug Show.*

Since the show is not juried and does not have special categories, rug hookers are encouraged to bring in all of their latest creations. Over one hundred hooked pieces are displayed at the one day show and enjoyed by a steady stream of visitors. *Courtesy of the Newtown Hooked Rug Show*.

Cultural Expressions

Rug makers pick up their hooks and pay tribute to ethnic and cultural diversities.

"'Lima' is an amalgam of Peruvian design elements, not necessarily borrowed from textiles. I approached this piece in a very traditional sense, incorporating as many aspects of ancient Andean ideology and technique as possible. The background was selected to mimic cochineal dyes; the color plan based upon a camelid palette (colors of animals in the camel family), with sparse use of blue and green (highly valuable), for contrast and for the status it would bring to the bearer of the cloth. Pattern and color relationships were more important than using colors realistically. Color was typically uniform and flat, with a bold juxtaposition of contrasting colors and outlining to set shapes apart." Designed by Jane McGown Flynn. House of Price/ Charco pattern. Hooked by Susan Higgins. California. 2001. 36" x 14". *Courtesy of Susan Higgins.*

Inspired by a bark painting, "Mexicana" was hooked to commemorate a trip south of the border. Designed by Pearl McGown. W. Cushing and Company pattern. Hooked by Jean Harris Coon. California. 1998. 26" x 20". *Courtesy of Jean Harris Coon.*

Embellished with reeds, feathers, leather, and beads, "Kwakiutl Indian Mask" honors one of Canada's Native tribes from British Columbia. "I was attracted to this mask because of the striking primary colors and sharp lines. The masks are known for rigid curves that delineated nostrils, eyes, and lips by using contrasting colors, which adds form to the mask." Adapted from a Kwakiutl mask. Hooked by Susan Mackey. Vermont. 2002. 13" x 9". *Courtesy of Susan Mackey.*

Symbolic of the Grand Canyon, "Marble Canyon" depicts Shivwits Indian motifs. The rug's center field represents the white marble found in the canyon. Included are four prayer sticks, two water spiders, directional triangles, and small arrow heads. Larger arrow heads are found on the border. Designed by Jane McGown Flynn. House of Price / Charco pattern. Hooked by Joan Reckwerdt. Oregon. 1997. 28" x 44". *Courtesy of Joan Reckwerdt.*

"Having worked for years with Navajo weaver Laura Florence in New Mexico, Navajo rugs and designs are also part of my household and memory. The 'Chief's Blanket' and its evolution has always been a favorite of mine because of the contrast of intense colors with black and white. This particular pattern was loosely adapted from a simple coin purse." Hooked from recycled woolen fabrics cut 6/32" wide. Hooked by Kathy T. Stephens. Montana. 2003. 13.5" x 19.5". *Courtesy of Kathy T. Stephens.*

—— Suzi Prather – Orlando, Florida ——

Popularized by "snow birds" (those that travel south to escape the icy blast of winter), rug hooking is alive, well, and thriving in Florida. With the area's balmy year round climate, there is really no need to make rugs to warm drafty floors, yet the Sunshine state is home to many contemporary rug hooking artists. Suzi Prather's mother and grandmother both hooked rugs, and since 2000, this talented Floridian has followed her family's tradition.

Using woolen fabric cut into strips 7/32" and 8/32" wide, Suzi Prather hooked "Red and Yellow, Black and White." "For this rug I traced the hands of my family and some of my friends. My mom is represented by the hand wearing a wedding band, as she and my dad were married over fifty years." Adapted from "Red and Yellow, Black and White." Designed by Pat Hornafius. Hooked by Suzi Prather. Florida. 2001. 32" x 45". *Courtesy of Suzi Prather.*

"Freedom – Don't Tread On Me." "After the events of 9/11, I wanted to make a patriotic rug—something to memorialize that event and our country's history. The flag that is folded into a triangle is in honor of my father and all the other World War II veterans." Much of the woolen fabric used to hook this commemorative work was hand-dyed by the artist. Designed and hooked by Suzi Prather. Florida. 2003. 34" x 43". *Courtesy of Suzi Prather.*

"I love fall and the shapes and colors of pumpkins." The dark blue midnight sky complements and intensifies the colors used to hook "Autumn Eve." The "02" date indicates the year the rug was started. The rug was completed the following year. Designed and hooked by Suzi Prather. Florida. 2003. 26" x 31". *Courtesy of Suzi Prather.*

"My friend, Barbara, is in her mid-70s and is one of the most fun people to be with. She is an inspiration, and no matter her 'age' she will never be old. It's an honor that she loves this rug." "Barb – Always a Fun Girl." Designed and hooked by Suzi Prather. Florida. 2004. 34.5" x 28". *Courtesy of Suzi Prather.*

"Our son and his wife were married in a beautiful park in downtown Orlando. The bride arrived, looking like a princess, in a horse-drawn carriage. After the ceremony, they departed in the carriage. I have tried to capture the moment of that beautiful day in 'Nathan and Theresa Get Married.'" Designed and hooked by Suzi Prather. Florida. 2004. 25" x 27". *Courtesy of Suzi Prather.*

A self portrait, hooked with strips of woolen fabric cut 6/32" and 7/32" wide, proclaims "Suzi – Has So Much Fun Playin' Hookey." "I enjoyed being able to see myself with fuller lips and fewer wrinkles." Designed and hooked by Suzi Prather. Florida. 2005. 12.5" x 11". *Courtesy of Suzi Prather.*

"Wanna Play?" "My black lab, Abbey, loves to play and have fun. She sits at the top of the stairs and bounces tennis balls down to me. She can always put two tennis balls in her mouth and on rare occasions has put three balls in, but that is not a very pretty sight." Designed and hooked by Suzi Prather. Florida. 2005. 47" x 33". *Courtesy of Suzi Prather.*

Doodlin' with Annie Spring

Having hooked and taught rug hooking for most of her life, Annie Spring continues to explore her chosen art form. Inspired by nature, whatever "catches my eye," and a good dose of imagination, the Massachusetts octogenarian is creating an array of appealing abstract designs. Named for her childhood days when her uncle, Ralph Burnham, antique dealer and "Hooked Rug Magnate," would go on buying trips and "tuck away" his tiny niece in the company truck, "Anne Tuckaway Doodlin' Motifs" are hooked with a variety of materials including woolen fabrics and a wide assortment of yarns. "Using tetrad color balance (a grouping of four) throughout, there is always balance and harmony in whatever the design may be. No specific drawings are needed. Doodlin' has no beginning and no end, as it is aimless." Relaxing and inspirational, "as you hook, you never know what images might develop. What starts out as abstract often turns realistic."

"Finding Your Way" combines traditional Celtic motifs, the look of illuminated stained glass, and a palette contemporary for the times. Note the gradual and near seamless color change in the finely shaded butterfly wings. David Rankine collection. Rittermere-Hurst-Field pattern. Hooked by Annie A. Spring. 1970. 17" x 17". *Courtesy of Annie A. Spring.*

Designed as an aid for color balance "Anne Tuckaway Doodlin' Motif #42" explores the varying intensities of a limited color scheme. Hooked with assorted yarns. Designed and hooked by Annie A. Spring. Massachusetts. 1997. 12" x 15". *Courtesy Annie A. Spring.*

"Burnham Floral" pays tribute to Annie Spring's uncle, Ralph Burnham. Owner of the Ipswich, Massachusetts Trading Post and dubbed the "Hooked Rug Magnate," Burnham advertised an inventory of over 3,000 rugs and was responsible for carpeting the homes of many notable clients, including the du Ponts and Wanamakers during the early 1900s. In later years, it was in his shop that the very young Annie learned to hook rugs. She patterned "Burnham Floral" after the center motif of "Burnham Legacy," a rug originally hooked in the 1880s and displayed at the Metropolitan Museum of Art in New York. Hooked by Annie A. Spring. Massachusetts. 1989. 32" x 48". *Courtesy of Annie A. Spring.*

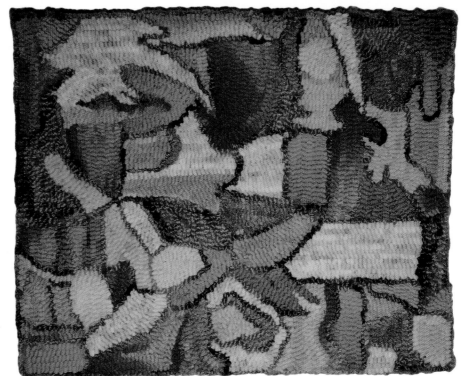

Paying careful attention to the placement of each color, shapes, of a somewhat structured nature, are restrained by contouring outlines. "Anne Tuckaway Doodlin' Motif #47." Hooked with assorted yarns. Designed and hooked by Annie A. Spring. Massachusetts. 1997. 11.5" x 14". *Courtesy of Annie A. Spring.*

When one takes a second look, ghostly images appear among the abstract motifs. "Anne Tuckaway Doodlin' Motif #73." Hooked with assorted yarns. Designed and hooked by Annie A. Spring. Massachusetts. 1999. 13" x 27". *Courtesy of Annie A. Spring.*

By hooking an off center, cross-like design, Annie Spring suggests a religious tone, thereby exalting her impressionistic and fragmented shards of "light." "Explosion 2000 – Anne Tuckaway Doodlin' Motif #21A." Hooked with assorted yarns. Designed and hooked by Annie A. Spring. Massachusetts. 2000. 11.5" x 14.5". *Courtesy of Annie A. Spring.*

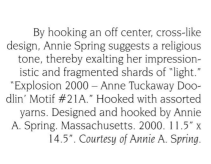

Hooked Horses

Horses, horses, horses...the mane event for many of today's rug hookers.

"I designed this rug for the entry of a new home. All the wool is from my old 'corporate' suits and those of my husband's. I felt it fitting, since 'Parchesi Horse' is in the entrance of our 'retirement' home! My husband thinks the suits never looked better." Designed and hooked by Lisanne Miller. Maine. 2005. 23" x 33". *Courtesy of Lisanne Miller.*

"My daughter, Maddie, is passionate about horses, so it was a must that I make a wall hanging for her room with horses on it." "Playful Ponies" was hooked with "mostly found" woolen fabrics, except for the sky, which was hand-dyed. Designed and hooked by Eugenie S. Delaney. Vermont. 2002. 21" x 31". *Courtesy of Eugenie S. Delaney.*

Well...that's "A Horse of a Different Color." Flanked by stars and framed by three corner fan motifs, this folk-art horse was hooked with tweeds and plaids. Woolley Fox pattern. Hooked by Gail Duclos Lapierre. Vermont. 2004. 14" x 26". *Courtesy of Gail Duclos Lapierre.*

Recalling an illustration in "one of my horse books which was given by my mother for my eighth birthday," galloping steeds rush to answer "The Alarm." "I've never forgotten those big, white horses racing to a fire." Designed and hooked by Jean Conrad Johnson. Vermont. 1995. 27" x 33". *Courtesy of Jean Conrad Johnson.*

"A dynamic buckskin Morgan-Arab, 'Topaz' was my daughter's first jumping horse; she loved to move. The equine design is adapted from a small metal brooch received as a gift, while the sun is an experiment based on Stonehenge-era cave symbols. Mountains, sky, and border are personal designs. Hooking with leather works well for lettering but I really began to dislike it throughout the body of the horse since it is so unforgiving and inelastic. 'Topaz' was hooked during various horse shows throughout Montana." Designed and hooked by Kathy T. Stephens. Montana. 2003. 11" x 15". *Courtesy of Kathy T. Stephens.*

"Of course I had to hook our other jumping horse and found a great brown tweed that inspired both him and this piece. Still working with leather, my goals were to give him a totally leather mane and tail. Also, when searching for wool in Butte, Montana second hand stores, I saw palm trees in a 'unique' old plaid coat. Since my daughter's trainer had gone to Florida to work the winter show season, why not send 'Lord Calvert' there in his rug?" Designed and hooked by Kathy T. Stephens. Montana. 2003. 12" x 16". *Courtesy of Kathy T. Stephens.*

To Delight Any Child

It has been said that to stay young at heart you should never lose the child within. Rug hookers embrace that ideology and create hooked works of art to delight any child, young or old.

Hooked Russian "Nesting Dolls," a colorful reminder of a trip to Moscow. Heart In Hand Pattern. Hooked by Fran Romig. Pennsylvania. 2000. 24" x 36". *Courtesy of Fran Romig.*

What child would not love this hooked treat? "Gingerbread." R.E.O. Design pattern. Hooked by Hildegard Edling. New York. 2002. 21" x 29". *Courtesy of Hildegard Edling.*

A diminutive "Sebastian" was hooked with woolen fabric cut 3/32" wide. Designed by Victoria Hart Ingalls. Victoria Hart Ingalls pattern. Hooked by JoAn Woody. Missouri. 2000. 9" x 6". *Courtesy of JoAn Woody.*

"I was to become a great-grandmother and needed a nursery rug to hook. Victoria Ingalls designed this rug using all of her precious bears lined up in a row." "Victoria's Bears." Victoria Hart Ingalls pattern. Hooked by Patricia J. Chambers. Missouri. 2004. 21" x 37". *Courtesy of Patricia J. Chambers.*

A former teddy bear collector de-clutters and preserves her memories by hooking a likeness of her stuffed friends. A moose joins the cuddly group, which includes a stylish bear wearing the tiara presented to the artist on her 50th birthday. "Basket of Bears." Designed by Vicki Darlington. Hooked by Patricia Laska. Maine. 2001. 22.5" x 31". *Courtesy of Patricia Laska.*

Dishes fly as Mr. Frog goes on a wild ride. "Hare Brained Idea." Pris Buttler Rug Designs pattern. Hooked by Hildegard Edling. New York. 2001. 29" x 38" *Courtesy of Hildegard Edling.*

The 1910 book, *Flower Children*, "is a part of my childhood, as my oldest sister read it to me frequently." With permission of Random House, Inc., who is now reprinting the vintage favorite, Nancy Thompson hooked likenesses of the "Flower Children" she so loved. Adapted from *Flower Children* by Elizabeth Gordon and illustrated by M. T. Ross. Hooked by Nancy Thompson. Georgia. 2003. Diameter 30". *Courtesy of Nancy Thompson and Random House Inc.*

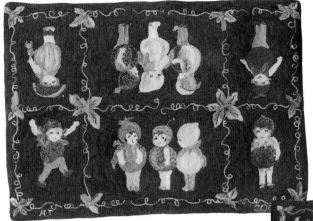

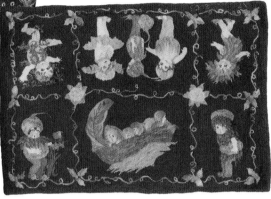

"I spent many hours pouring over the pages of *Mother Earth's Children* when I was a little girl in the 1940s." With permission of Random House Inc., who is reprinting the 1914 classic, "Fruit Babies," Vegetable Babies," and "Nut Babies" have once again come to life thanks to Nancy Thompson's magic hook. Adapted from *Mother Earth's Children* by Elizabeth Gordon. Illustrated by M.T. Ross. Hooked by Nancy Thompson. Georgia. 2003. 2005. 2003. 36" x 60; 36" x 60"; 36" x 52". *Courtesy of Nancy Thompson and Random House Inc.*

Hooked to commemorate the birth of a special nephew. "I wanted the rug to be suitable for a boy or a girl and also not to be too "babyish." Wyatt Hugh Manuell Stetler was born the day the rug was completed. "Alphabet." Designed and hooked by Jennifer Manuell. Ontario, Canada. 2000. 41" x 52". *Courtesy of Jennifer Manuell.*

"Son Up – Son Down." "This rug was made for my sister, Joan Valley. She is a wonderful mother and I appreciate, more then she will ever know, her allowing me to share in Noah's and Carter's lives." Hooked with various yarns, "favorite things," including a dolphin, football, race car, and pumpkin, surround the bathing duo. Designed and hooked by Peggy J. Mineau. Wisconsin. 2003. 20" x 26". *Courtesy of Peggy J. Mineau.*

"Hooked for my great-nephew, Ryan," the stage is set for more than a three-ring circus. In addition to hooking with woolen fabric, the artist used yarn embellishments in the clown's and gypsy's hair, the dog's fur, and the horse's mane and tail. "The Circus." Designed by Bruce Horvath with additions by Diane Stoffel. Hooked by Susan Naples. California. 2004. 22" x 53.5". *Courtesy of Susan Naples.*

Details of "The Circus." *Courtesy of Susan Naples.*

Nursery rhyme characters form a frame around a beloved "Mother Goose." Detail and fine shading were achieved by hooking with woolen fabric cut 3/32" and 4/32" wide. Designed by Victoria Hart Ingalls. Victoria Hart Ingalls pattern. Hooked by Minerva D. Cabanas. Kansas. 2004. 30" x 38". *Courtesy of Minerva D. Cabanas.*

"I saved this drawing for close to thirty years and thought it would be fun to hook." "How Dear to My Heart." Designed by Erika and Diane Neuse with help from Beverly Conway. Hooked by Diane Neuse. Vermont. 2002. 36" x 24". *Courtesy of Diane Neuse.*

"Having done one already for her sister (Erika) I had to do #2 for Kirsten. She was 6 when she did the drawing. She is now 37." "How Dear to My Heart #2." Designed by Kirsten and Diane Neuse. Hooked by Diane Neuse. Vermont. 2003. 36" x 24". *Courtesy of Diane Neuse.*

"I hook a lot of rugs and am always looking for subjects. I saw this 1924 children's activity book at a garage sale and the lights came on in my head. Let's play. The book is charming and well used. McLoughlin Bros. Publishers are long out of business but the artwork of Louise Tessin will live on in this rug." "Something To Do." Adapted from an illustration by Louise Tessin in *Something To Do for Every Day*. Hooked by Ruth Hennessey. New York. 2004. 28" x 24". *Courtesy of Ruth Hennessey.*

"Annie," huggable hooked art. "I took the standard Raggedy Ann doll pattern, elongated the torso a little, and altered the apron some too. Her head was hooked front and back with the same wool out of which I made the doll." Adapted from a Raggedy Ann doll pattern. Hooked by Victoria Hart Ingalls. Missouri. 1997. 21" tall. *Courtesy of Victoria Hart Ingalls.*

Detail of "Something To Do." *Courtesy of Ruth Hennessey.*

Rhapsody in Rugs –
Rags to Rugs at the Carnegie

Believing that rich men are "trustees" of their wealth and should administer it for the good of the public, Andrew Carnegie (1835-1919) would surely have been pleased to know that the Carnegie Center for Art and History in New Albany, Indiana was the first in the area to host a juried exhibition of hooked rugs. Originally crafted from discarded clothing and fabrics, hooked rugs were a thrifty way of warming drafty floors. This fact alone would have

brought a smile to the American industrialist and kindly philanthropist of Scottish heritage.

On display at the exhibition were the works of hooking artists from across the United States and Canada. The two-month long show attracted a large and enthusiastic audience. The following are selections from the 2005 exhibit.

All rug photos by Myra Silva.

Gecko Dreams
Laurie Wiles
40"x52"

Announcing the 2005 first annual *Rhapsody in Rugs* exhibit at the Carnegie Center for Art and History in New Albany, Indiana. Co-sponsored by New Albany's Cat House Rugs and sanctioned by ATHA (Association of Traditional Hooking Artist), the two-month long event offered rug hooking classes and workshops, with a changing roster of teachers and programs. *Courtesy of the Carnegie Center for Art and History.*

A seated Jyl Clark, hooking artist and co-owner of New Albany's Cat House Rugs, and Vermont hooking artist and teacher Stephanie Krauss were on hand to greet visitors at the opening of *Rhapsody in Rugs*. *Courtesy of the Carnegie Center for Art and History.*

"Friendship and Hospitality." Capri Boyle Jones. 56" x 44". *Courtesy of the Carnegie Center for Art and History.*

"Nova Scotia Cove." Anne Stevens. 25" x 34". *Courtesy of the Carnegie Center for Art and History.*

"Autumn Bouquet." Christine Parker. 36" x 36". *Courtesy of the Carnegie Center for Art and History.*

Old Key West II. John Flournoy. 25" x 51". *Courtesy of the Carnegie Center for Art and History.*

"Patterson Oriental." Judy McKinley. 36" x 72". *Courtesy of the Carnegie Center for Art*

Above left:
"Patchwork Pumpkin." Leslie O. Norton. 26"
x 35". *Courtesy of the Carnegie Center for Art and History.*

Above right:
"Greyhound." Linda Harwood. 16" x 21".
Courtesy of the Carnegie Center for Art and History.

Left:
"Samsara." Natasha Chan. 67" x 39". *Courtesy of the Carnegie Center for Art and History.*

"It's a Keeper." Pat Van Arsdale. 30" x 50". *Courtesy of the Carnegie Center for Art and History.*

"Caswell Fruit." Sheri Bennett. 31" x 73". *Courtesy of the Carnegie Center for Art and History.*

"The Collection." Wendy Miller. 60" x 42". *Courtesy of the Carnegie Center for Art and History.*

173

A Spiritual Side

Getting in touch with one's spiritual side is an awakening process for many of today's hooking artists.

Among Native people, the hawk has long been considered a spiritual "Messenger." Designed and hooked by Jan Seavey. New Hampshire. 1997. 14" x 12". *Courtesy of Jan Seavey.*

"Back in the mid 90s, I was at an antique store with my daughter. I saw a beautiful green velvet cape with a gold satin lining. I touched it and felt a strange sensation. I was hesitant to try it on. The shop owner and my daughter insisted. As I tried it on a vision came over me, like I was transported back in time. As I turned around, with tears in my eyes, to look at my daughter, she also had tears in her eyes. She had the same vision. We were stunned and the shop lady was a bit spooked. We left and went home. An hour later a friend called me requesting some art work so I went over to her house. As I walked in the cape was hanging over her door jam. The shop owner had called and told her what had happened…they were friends and my friend knew I had to have that cape.

"In my vision I was standing on a hillside with the full moon at my back. I had a hawk on a staff and a wolf at my feet. The wind was blowing and my cape was blown open. Hooked on the top of my rug are Ogham letters, a secret language used by Druids to pass on tales. It reads 'I AM WHO I AM.' The side borders are the Runic alphabet, the bottom design was borrowed from a bracelet I purchased in Scotland." "Inner Remembering." Designed and hooked by Jan Seavey. New Hampshire. 2005. 35" x 27". *Courtesy of Jan Seavey.*

The bald eagle symbolizes a "Sacred Spirit." Designed and hooked by Jan Seavey. New Hampshire. 1998. 12" x 14". *Courtesy of Jan Seavey.*

"The Spirit of My Hollow Tree." "Behind my house is an ancient hollow maple tree that I dearly love. I visit it often and give it words of encouragement as it is on the last leg of its life. It has a wonderful hollow area that is big enough for me to stand in. When I stand in it, I am a little girl all over again, maybe even an elf or a fairy." Designed and hooked by Suzanne Dirmaier. Vermont. 2003. 31.5" x 26". *Courtesy of Suzanne Dirmaier.*

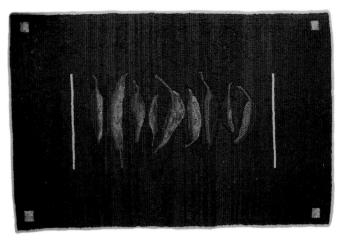

"Meditation Rug," the first of a series of Asian-inspired designs based on various forms of nature, offers mindfully placed red leaves. Designed and hooked by Polly Alexander. Vermont. 2000. 21" x 31". *Courtesy of Polly Alexander.*

The "Zodiac" signs of family members are framed by whimsical meteorological and astronomical symbols. Designed and hooked by Diane Moore. Vermont. 2001. 22" x 36". *Courtesy of Diane Moore.*

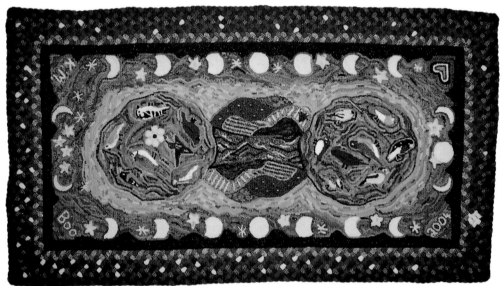

In Buddhist culture, a bodhisattva is a being who brings enlightenment to all. Tribute is paid to the spirit of Bodhi, a very special dog. "We pictured him in the stars. He loved being outside during all seasons." Vermont birds flank a cross cut tree section framed by winding roads. "The Boo Rug." Designed and hooked by Kris McDermet. Vermont. 2004. 27" x 50". *Courtesy of Kris McDermet.*

In celebration of the Day of the Dead, many people of Mexican heritage follow the tradition of adorning altars with food, drink, flowers, and trinkets to entice departed souls to visit and share in the offerings. In preparation for such an altar, this piece, using Mexican iconography and traditional colors, was hooked to honor the artist's parents. "La Travesia – The Crossing Over." Designed and hooked by Tricia Tague Miller. New Hampshire. 2002. 14.5" x 14.5". *Courtesy of Tricia Tague Miller.*

A Biblical verse frames two stately homes. Blue birds of happiness fly over the scene. "Sampler of Faith." Pris Buttler Rug Designs pattern. Hooked by Lee Abrego. New Hampshire. 2002. 52" x 32". *Courtesy of Lee Abrego.*

John and Nancy Ewbank –
Bartlesville, Oklahoma

For nine months during 1995, while his wife was still working, the retired John Ewbank traveled each Thursday from Parsons, Kansas, to Independence, Missouri, to take rug hooking lessons from Victoria Hart Ingalls. With no super highways available, the scenic but slow 216 mile round trip through small country towns took six hours and forty minutes. "I was the only man in the class but the ladies made me feel welcomed. I learned a lot and made many friends." Informed about rug hooking camps, John began his tradition of attending one yearly. As his passion grew, he "bugged" his wife, Nancy, to take up rug hooking. Her standard reply was "No thanks." Eventually, enticed by a sterling silver hook made by Victoria's husband Tom, and given as a gift if she would promise to make just one rug, the once reluctant Nancy was "hooked."

In 2002, the Ewbanks moved to Oklahoma and have been hooking together ever since.

After nine months of driving thousands of miles to take rug hooking classes in another state, John Ewbank completed "Fruitful Harvest." "One day while hooking, one of the ladies (in class) said I had everything in the rug except a lady bug so we added one. It made the rug complete. Insects, fruit, and ribbon tied it all together." Designed by Victoria Hart Ingalls. Victoria Hart Ingalls pattern. Hooked by John Ewbank. Oklahoma. 1995. 43" x 49". *Courtesy of John E. Ewbank.*

"Iris Wreath" was John's first attempt at hooking flowers. Designed by Mildred Sprout. Hooked by John Ewbank. Oklahoma. 1996. 32" x 41". *Courtesy of John E. Ewbank.*

Nancy and John Ewbank stand beside "Emma Dean." Custom designed, the pattern for this rug was never named or used. After John finished hooking it, he thought it only proper to name the rug after the woman it was originally designed for. Designed by Margaret Hunt Masters. Hooked by John Ewbank. Oklahoma. 1999. 44" x 78". *Courtesy of John E. Ewbank.*

John Ewbank began work on "Emma Dean" in March of 1995. Due to illness, the project was completed four years later. "It proved to be the most challenging and inspirational work of anything I have ever hooked so far." The reverse image area-sized rug was hooked with many hand-dyed woolen fabric swatches. The background color was specially dyed to coordinate with carpeting in the Ewbanks' home. Designed by Margaret Hunt Masters. Hooked by John Ewbank. Oklahoma. 1999. 44" x 78". Photo by Sherry L. Stinson / Tyler Creative. *Courtesy of John E. Ewbank.*

Details of "Emma Dean." The fruit, vegetables, and cornucopias were hooked with hand-dyed woolen fabric cut 3/32" wide. By using a fine cut, John achieved life-like shading and detail. Photos by Sherry L. Stinson / Tyler Creative. *Courtesy of John E. Ewbank.*

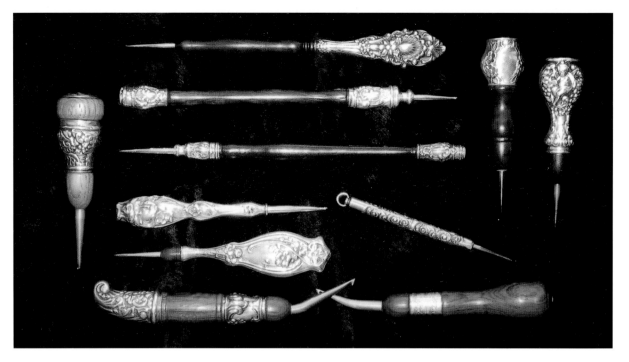

Samples of the sterling silver handled hooks made by Tom Ingalls, the likes of which enticed Nancy Ewbank to hook her first rug. *Courtesy of Tom Ingalls.*

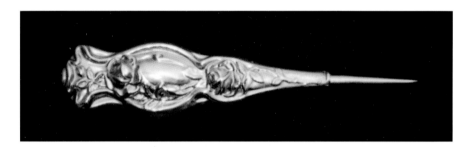

Nancy Ewbank's own rose motif, sterling silver handled hook. *Courtesy of Nancy Ewbank.*

Although she was reluctant for years to even try hooking, Nancy Ewbank's "Sheeps in the Meadow" was a fun and successful first project. Designed by Kathy Morton. Hooked by Nancy Ewbank. Oklahoma. 1999. 17" x 23". *Courtesy of Nancy C. Ewbank.*

Having told his hooking instructor, Nancy Blood, that his favorite color was green, John Ewbank was surprised when he arrived at rug camp to find not one shade of green among the swatches she had hand-dyed for him to hook "Harmony." "'Trust me,' she said. "I thought 'what the heck,' I might as well give it a try. She was right. After it was hooked, the green showed up. I have trusted her ever since. What a masterpiece of color." Designed by Jane McGown Flynn. House of Price / Charco pattern. Hooked by John Ewbank. Oklahoma. 2001. 36" x 70". *Courtesy of John E. Ewbank.*

At her first rug camp, using "my beautiful silver handled hook," Nancy Ewbank fashioned her second rug, "For Idle Moments." Designed by Pearl McGown. W. Cushing and Company pattern. Hooked by Nancy Ewbank. Oklahoma. 2002. 30" x 50". *Courtesy of Nancy C. Ewbank.*

Idyllic Landscapes

Ahhhhh...peace and tranquility. Rug hookers create idyllic settings.

Using strips of woolen faric cut 6/32" wide, Suzanne Hamer achieved a painterly quality when she hooked "At the River's Bend." Designed by Jane McGown Flynn. House of Price / Charco pattern. Hooked by Suzanne S. Hamer. Illinois. 1996. 11" x 14.5". *Courtesy of Suzanne S. Hamer*

"Summer in New England" captures the essence of country living. Note how subtle tonal changes in color help create perspective and depth in the various buildings. Designed by Jane McGown Flynn. House of Price / Charco pattern. Hooked by Suzanne S. Hamer. Illinois. 2003. 12" x 16". *Courtesy of Suzanne S. Hamer.*

The difficult job of conveying where the water ends and the sky begins was successfully mastered by Suzanne Hamer. Still waters offer a faint reflection of the red-roofed cabin on "Summer Lake." Designed by Jane McGown Flynn. House of Price / Charco pattern. Hooked by Suzanne S. Hamer. Illinois. 1996. 11" x 14". *Courtesy of*

Smokey, the schnauzer, romps under a bright stylized sun in "Liebchen's Garden." Designed by Nan Carpenter. Hooked by Margot A. Morrison. Georgia. 2004. 22" x 40". *Courtesy of Margot A. Morrison.*

"Forest Gatherings" of winter berries are contained in a wicker basket placed in an imagined setting where dense woodland mushrooms and ferns meet with sun loving flowers and butterflies. Designed and hooked by Karen Goulart. Rhode Island. 2003. 22" x 29". *Courtesy of Karen Goulart.*

A wooden sash serves as a frame and as a "Picture Window," offering us this countryside view from a cat's perspective. Woolen fabrics cut in a variety of widths were used to hook the scene. Designed by Jane Olson. Hooked by Cathe Evans. Missouri. 2004. 24" x 36". *Courtesy of Cathe Evans.*

Recalling another era with a pastoral scene of the "Little Red School House." Designed by Jane Olson. Hooked by Dorothy Rezac. Kansas. 2004. Diameter 14". *Courtesy of Dorothy Rezac.*

"Echoes of the Past," the hooking artist's rendition of an ideal home. Designed and hooked by Jan Seavey. New Hampshire. 2005. 17" x 30". *Courtesy of Jan Seavey.*

Hooking Angels

There are angels amongst us. Many rug hookers feel strongly about this belief, and hook likenesses of these celestial and spiritual beings.

"My Hooking Mentor" is a tribute to rug hooking artist and teacher, Canada's own Jean Armstrong, or Auntie Jean, as she is known to Jennifer Manuell. In addition to Jean teaching her niece how to hook, Jean and Jennifer are kindred spirits. Depicted are some of the interests they both share: books, wool, and the process of dyeing as represented by a wok full of fabric. The light bulb symbolizes ideas and the stars encouragement. An owl, a favorite feathered friend, stands for Jean's business savvy. Also portrayed is her cat, a faithful and constant companion. Presented to Jean on her 75th birthday. Designed and hooked by Jennifer Manuell. Ontario, Canada. 2002. 36" x 27.5". *Courtesy of Jennifer Manuell.*

Reiki is an ancient healing technique used for transferring energy from the giver to the receiver. Kathleen Betts Boozan, believing in heavenly beings, hooked this rug to honor all the Reiki angels that bring love. "Flying Angel." Designed and hooked by Kathleen Betts Boozan. Vermont. 2004. 24" x 31". *Courtesy of Kathleen Betts Boozan.*

A banner proclaiming "Peace To All" forms a protective dome over a sleepy country village as three guardian "Angels on High" keep watch. New Earth Designs pattern. Hooked by Doris Hennessy. Maine. 2004. 16" x 30". *Courtesy of Doris Hennessy.*

To benefit their church bazaar, parishioners were asked to create an angel using their favorite craft. Ceil Murdoch drew this celestial being flying above the churches of Middlebury, Vermont, and Diane Neuse hooked the early evening scene. When the piece was auctioned off, knowing Diane's and her children's fondness for the rug, an anonymous friend placed the winning bid on Diane's behalf. The church coffers were handsomely rewarded and Diane and her children were delighted. "Twilight In Middlebury, Vermont." Designed by Ceil Murdoch. Hooked by Diane Neuse. Vermont. 2004. 17" x 30". *Courtesy of Diane Neuse.*

A simplistic and charming "Stained Glass Angel." Designed by Jeanne Stewart. Hooked by Dorothy Rezac. Kansas. 2004. 10" x 8". *Courtesy of Dorothy Rezac.*

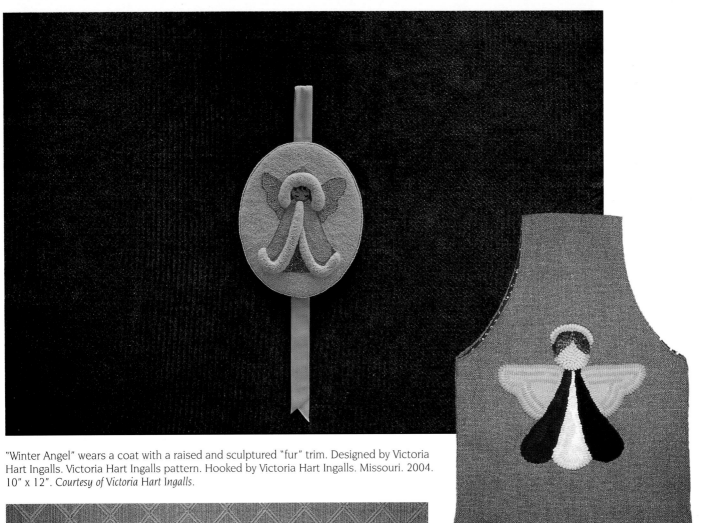

"Winter Angel" wears a coat with a raised and sculptured "fur" trim. Designed by Victoria Hart Ingalls. Victoria Hart Ingalls pattern. Hooked by Victoria Hart Ingalls. Missouri. 2004. 10" x 12". *Courtesy of Victoria Hart Ingalls.*

Originally designed for a pin, the image of "Patriotic Angel" was enlarged and hooked directly onto this tote bag. Designed by Victoria Hart Ingalls. Victoria Hart Ingalls pattern. Hooked by Victoria Hart Ingalls. Missouri. 2003. 16" x 12". *Courtesy of Victoria Hart Ingalls.*

Angels can always find your keys. Designed by Victoria Hart Ingalls. Victoria Hart Ingalls pattern. Hooked by Victoria Hart Ingalls. Missouri. 1998. 4" x 10.5". *Courtesy of Victoria Hart Ingalls.*

And…yes, there are angels in "Hog Heaven." "I thought it would be fun if everything was pink!" Designed by Linda Pietz. Cactus Needle pattern. Hooked by Nola A. Heidbreder. Missouri. 2004. 23" x 30.5". *Courtesy of Nola A. Heidbreder.*

Heart of Texas

San Antonio Chapter of ATHA (Association of Traditional Hooking Artists)

Members of San Antonio's Heart of Texas chapter of ATHA had a goal to design and hook an "eclectic" rug. The rug had to be unique, "composed of elements drawn from various sources" and something that people would remember.

Patterned after a flower, the "Heart of Texas Rug" was designed with sixteen petals, each depicting themes of the Lone Star state. The graphics were transferred to hooking linen and volunteers stepped forward to work on the individual petals. Once completed, each was sewn around the Heart of Texas center. Presented at the 2004, 3rd Annual Angela Pumphrey Weekend Rug Hooking Workshop at the Hilton San Antonio Airport Hotel, this special rug will be exhibited throughout the United States and Canada and used to promote rug hooking as an art form.

"Heart of Texas Rug." Designed by Stephanie Latham. Graphics by Anita L. McFarland. The following were hooked by: "Cowgirl Angel"– Angela Pumphrey; "Sunflower"– Barbara Westwood; "Cactus" – Jo Thompson; "Texas Flag"– Gladys Cain; "Dogwood"– Kathy Fleming Korvic; "Oil Derrick" – Sandra Sigler; "Chili Pepper" –Stephanie Latham; "Longhorn and Hat"– Kathy Fleming Korvic; "Bird and Berries" – Bea Brock; "Alamo"– Betty Will; "Stripes"– Joan Dixon; "Bluebonnets"– Carol Gillingham; "Stars"– Anita L. McFarland; "Guitar"– Boni Roe; "Texas Seal"– Loyce Kahil; "Sun"– Maureen Arrow; "Heart of Texas Center"– Anita L. McFarland. Texas. 2004. Diameter 60". *Courtesy of the* ATHA *Heart of Texas chapter. San Antonio, Texas.*

Americana

Rug makers raise their hooks and salute the red, white, and blue.

"Patriotic Morning." An American flag complements the faint silhouette of a weathervane rooster. "I wanted to try the 'transparent' effect of one image over another. The biggest challenge was selecting the wools that would achieve this effect." Designed and hooked by Karen Cooper. New Hampshire. 2003. 20" x 24.5". *Courtesy of Karen Cooper.*

The flag flies and home fires burn at "Liberty Cabin." Note the developing patterns in the contouring sky. Laurice Heath pattern. Hooked by Elizabeth Baier. Texas. 1995. 16" x 24". *Courtesy of Elizabeth Baier.*

"Bees and Trees" and the American flag compose this folk art collage. Strips of woolen fabric cut 8/32" wide were used to create an "antique" look in Diane Burgess' second rug. Vermont Folk Rugs pattern. Hooked by Diane Burgess. Vermont. 1999. 36" x 24". *Courtesy of Diane Burgess.*

Janine Williams expressed her patriotic feelings with word, date, eagle, flag, olive branches, and stars. "Liberty." Designed by Barb Adams. Hooked by Janine Williams. Texas. 2004. Diameter 27". *Courtesy of Janine Williams.*

Adapted from a section of a centennial Baltimore quilt, a firecracker and stylized stars and shield were added to a traditional design. Plaids were used to hook the side panels. Jacqueline Designs pattern. Hooked by Jacqueline Hansen. Maine. 2000. 26" x 36". *Courtesy of Jacqueline Hansen.*

Experienced quilt maker Janine Williams tried her hand at rug hooking by making a tiny tribute to the land of the red, white, and blue. "Patriotic Star." Designed and hooked by Janine Williams. Texas. 2004. 8" x 8.5". *Courtesy of Janine Williams.*

"Miss Liberal," the liberated cousin of New York's Miss Liberty, strikes a pose for modern women. Designed and hooked by Diane Kelly. Vermont. 1998. 50" x 19". *Courtesy of Diane Kelly.*

A hooked replica of the1851 Leutze painting of "George Washington" crossing the Delaware. Note how the tassel on the flag and part of an oar venture into the outer border. Pris Buttler Rug Designs pattern. Hooked by Lee Abrego. New Hampshire. 31" x 40". *Courtesy of Lee Abrego.*

"Old Glory" waves in the land of the free and the home of the brave. Woolen fabric strips cut 6/32", 7/32", and 8/32" wide were used to hook the stars and undulating stripes. The firecracker adds a celebratory note. Designed and hooked by Annie Wilson. California. 2003. 16" x 22". *Courtesy of Annie Wilson.*

Suggested Reading

Burton, Mary Sheppard. *A Passion for the Creative Life; Textiles to Lift the Spirit*. Edited by Mary Ellen Cooper. Germantown, Maryland: Sign of the Hook Books, 2002.

Carroll, Barbara. *American Folk Art Rug Hooking – 18 Art Projects with Rug Hooking Basics, Tips & Techniques*. Urbandale, Iowa: Laundauer Books, 2005.

Field, Jeanne. *Shading Flowers: The Complete Guide for Rug Hookers*. Harrisburg, Pennsylvania: Stackpole Books, 1991.

Lais, Emma Lou, and Barbara Carroll. *American Primitive Hooked Rugs: Primer for Re-creating Antique Rugs*. Kennebunkport, Maine: Wildwood Press, 1999.

Logsdon, Roslyn. *People and Places: Roslyn Logsdon's Imagery in Fiber*. Rug Hooking Magazine's Framework Series Edition. Harrisburg, Pennsylvania: David Detweiler.1998.

Mather, Anne D. *Creative Rug Hooking*. New York, New York: Sterling Company, 2000.

Moshimer, Joan. *Hooked on Cats: Complete Patterns and Instructions for Rug Hookers*. Harrisburg, Pennsylvania: Stackpole Books. 1991.

Moshimer, Joan. *The Complete Rug Hooker*. Boston: New York Graphic Society, 1975.

Oxford, Amy. *Hooked Rugs Today*. Atglen, Pennsylvania: Schiffer Publishing Ltd., 2005.

Oxford, Amy. *Punch Needle Rug Hooking: Techniques and Designs*. Atglen, Pennsylvania: Schiffer Publishing Ltd., 2003.

Thompson, Nancy Butts. *Hooking on the Hill*. Georgia: Nancy Butts Thompson, 2005.

Turbayne, Jessie A. *Hooked on Rugs: Outstanding Contemporary Designs*. Atglen, Pennsylvania: Schiffer Publishing Ltd., 2006.

Turbayne, Jessie A. *Hooked Rugs: History and the Continuing Tradition*. West Chester, Pennsylvania: Schiffer Publishing Ltd., 1991.

Turbayne, Jessie A. *Hooked Rug Treasury*. Atglen, Pennsylvania: Schiffer Publishing Ltd., 1997.

Turbayne, Jessie A. *The Big Book of Hooked Rugs*. Atglen, Pennsylvania: Schiffer Publishing Ltd., 2005.

Turbayne, Jessie A. *The Complete Guide to Collecting Hooked Rugs: Unrolling the Secrets*. Atglen, Pennsylvania: Schiffer Publishing Ltd., 2004.

Turbayne, Jessie A. *The Hooker's Art*. Atglen, Pennsylvania: Schiffer Publishing Ltd., 1993.

Yoder, Patty. *The Alphabet of Sheep*. Raleigh, North Carolina: Ivy House Publishing Group, 2003.